A Short History of the T.U.C.

A Short History of the T.U.C.

JOHN Christopher LOVELL
and
B. C. ROBERTS

MACMILLAN

© John Lovell and B. C. Roberts 1968

Published by
MACMILLAN AND CO LTD
Little Essex Street London WC2
and also at Bombay Calcutta and Madras
Macmillan South Africa (Publishers) Pty Ltd Johannesburg
The Macmillan Company of Australia Pty Ltd Melbourne
The Macmillan Company of Canada Ltd Toronto

Printed in Great Britain by
ROBERT MACLEHOSE AND CO LTD
University Press, Glasgow

Contents

Contents

1 The First Trades Union Congress, 1868

1. ATTEMPTS TO CREATE A NATIONAL ORGANISATION

THE Congress organised by The Manchester and Salford Trades
Council at the Mechanics Institute, Manchester, on 2 June 1868,
to discuss 'the present aspect of trade unions' has been followed in
almost unbroken annual succession over the last hundred years.
Today the T.U.C. is recognised on all sides as a body that represents the collective opinions of the great bulk of employees. Its
status is such that it is consulted by all governments on every issue
that is of public concern to workpeople; its representatives sit on a
great variety of public committees and councils; it speaks on behalf
of British trade unions in the international labour field. The views
of the trade unions that are gathered and formulated at the annual
congress are now given practical expression through a General
Council that meets monthly, and the General Secretary, assisted
by a permanent staff of national officers who carry out their duties
from Congress House, one of the most modern and impressive
buildings in the centre of London.

In short, the T.U.C. is much more than an annual parliament of
labour; it is a great national organisation exercising a powerful
and continuous influence on governments, employers and public
opinion that has become a vital element in the pluralist system of
democracy through which the British people govern themselves,
and an example followed in other countries all over the world. The
purpose of this book is to trace the growth and development of the
T.U.C. from its first tentative beginnings over a hundred years ago
to its present position of importance and authority.

A number of attempts were made to create nationwide trade-
union federations before the successful establishment of the Trades
Union Congress in 1868. In the years between 1829 and 1834 a
number of national trades conferences were organised by a cotton
spinner named John Doherty and the famous radical reformer
Robert Owen, but these efforts came to naught.

The fact was that economic, political and technical conditions were not yet sufficiently favourable to make a national organisation a feasible proposition. During the next few years the unions were compelled by adverse economic conditions to husband their limited resources and to concentrate on survival. Although the unions played little direct part in the agitation to secure parliamentary reforms that would benefit workers, their active members gave support to the Chartists.

In 1845 a 'National Association of United Trades for the Protection of Labour' was established to promote the well being of the associated trades by mediation, arbitration and legal proceedings and by the supporting of all political, social and educational measures which were designed to improve the 'condition of the labouring classes'. Unlike the earlier Owenite national associations this body was, in the words of the Webbs, 'distinguished by the moderation of its aims and the prudence of its administration.' Although this cautious and realistic policy enabled the National Association of United Trades for the Protection of Labour to survive for fifteen years and to score some modest, though not unimportant, successes, it attracted relatively little support from the unions. It can, however, be looked upon as a forerunner of the T.U.C.

As economic conditions improved and unions gradually built up their strength they began to press their challenge to the employers with greater vigour. The building trades in particular started to agitate for shorter hours and better wages. The demand for improved conditions of employment was crystallised in a struggle for a maximum working day of nine hours, which was most strongly pressed in London, but was extended over much of the country.

The conflict over the daily hours worked in the building industry erupted into bitter dispute when an employer dismissed some of his workers because they presented a petition in support of the unions' claim. The efforts of the employers to crush the unions by means of a lock-out convinced many, hitherto strong supporters of local unionism, that they must now follow the example of the Amalgamated Society of Engineers and combine to form strong nation-wide associations. At the same time, the builders' struggle created a sense of solidarity between the different trades and encouraged them to form trades councils to provide mutual aid and promote united action in defence of their common interests.

During the builders' dispute there had been weekly meetings of the metropolitan trades for the purpose of giving aid and organising support for the strikers. A few years earlier a London Committee of Metropolitan Trades Delegates had been established to support efforts that were then being made to raise a fund to help locked-out cotton operatives, but this had not survived. It was now decided to establish a London Trades Council. Similar bodies had already come into existence elsewhere and others were in the process of being set up. Within a short time Trades Councils were flourishing in Birmingham, Liverpool, Manchester, Sheffield and a number of other towns.

The growth of the nation-wide amalgamated societies with strong finances and a national leadership that was capable of visualising the role of the unions on a national scale, together with the development of local Trades Councils, were essential precursors to the establishment of the Trades Union Congress. Trade-union organisation on a national scale had been made much easier with the technical development of cheap and rapid communications, which began with the introduction of the penny-post system in the 1840s and the covering of Britain with an efficient network of railways. The need for a national organisation which would unite all the unions and press their common interests on the Government was not yet accepted, but events were soon to make its desirability obvious.

2. THE EMERGENCE OF NATIONAL LEADERS

The necessity to extend union organisation from the local basis had become increasingly obvious with the growth of industry in great urban centres, rising competition, and the development of mass markets that expanded and contracted in a violent and un-predictable fashion. These conditions had stimulated employers to counter the emerging strength of the trade unions with a more vigorous opposition. Advancing technology and economic growth thus combined to push trade unions and employers into making institutional responses that were more appropriate than the forms of union organisation and employer behaviour that had previously existed.

The general secretaries of the national amalgamated societies were quick to see that the London Trades Council offered them an opportunity to bring their influence to bear on issues that were of major concern to all the unions and they were soon playing a dominant role. William Allan, General Secretary of the Engineers, Robert Applegarth of the Carpenters and Joiners, Daniel Guile of the Ironfounders, Edwin Coulson of the Bricklayers acting in alliance with two remarkable leaders of small London societies, George Odger of the Ladies Shoemakers and George Howell of the Operative Bricklayers became, in the words of the Webbs, the 'informal cabinet of the trade-union world'.

The influence and authority of this group grew rapidly as the Council assumed responsibility for organising help to societies that appealed for aid when they were involved in strikes or lock-outs. In carrying out this function the leaders of the Council were careful to avoid encouraging the unions to adopt an aggressive and militant policy which they feared would invite retaliation and prove financially unbearable. The general secretaries of the amalgamated societies were all careful and cautious administrators who had built up their unions by husbanding their resources, and they were not prepared to support strikes until it could be shown that every other way of achieving a reasonable settlement of a union demand had been tried and found wanting.

This conservative policy did not meet with the approval of all the trade unions and it was particularly criticised by George Potter, Secretary of a small London union, the Progressive Society of Carpenters and Joiners.[1] Potter was a man of unusual ability. He had considerable talents as orator, writer and agitator, and had acquired a large following in the building trades. Potter had been mainly responsible for leading the unions in the nine-hour day strike and for organising an important conference of builders' union representatives at Derby in 1861. Through these activities Potter was probably better known throughout the country than any of the other trade union leaders.

The leaders of the London Trades Council looked upon Potter as an irresponsible agitator and he in turn looked upon them as bureaucratic, secretive and unduly cautious. In many respects, Potter represented the older concept of local trade unionism which was giving way before the more highly developed, centrally controlled, professionally administered, large-scale national amalgamated societies.

[1] For a full account of the activities of George Potter see B. C. Roberts, *The Trades Union Congress, 1868–1921* (1958).

Differences in personality also separated Potter from men like Allan and Applegarth. Potter enjoyed the limelight and the convivial life of the militant local leader; Allan and Applegarth were made of different stuff and they looked with contempt on leadership exercised from the public house bar and the street corner soapbox. In the eyes of the leaders of the amalgamated societies, respectability through responsibility was the key to the future role of the unions; in Potter's view the unions were only likely to earn the respect of employers and the Government by demonstrating their strength through militant industrial and political activities.

In pursuit of his aims to promote a vigorous trade union policy Potter launched a newspaper in 1861 which he called *The Beehive*. With some reluctance the leaders of the London Trades Council were persuaded to support the paper, but they were never happy at being in the position of having no control over the editor and they eventually severed their connection with the paper.

This distrust of Potter was soon confirmed when the editor of *The Beehive*, in their opinion, perversely decided to support the Southern Confederacy in the American Civil War. Potter's reason for taking this position was that a victory for the North would be damaging to Britain's trade interests, since the Southern States were natural trading partners exporting cotton and tobacco and taking British manufactures in return, whereas the North was bent on keeping British goods out by high tariffs. The leaders of the London Trades Council would not accept this line of argument, since, in their opinion, loss of trade advantage could not offset the moral claim of the North for trade union support on the issue of slavery. Almost as damaging was the fact that Potter's position aligned him with the British Government which had come perilously close to intervening on the side of the South.

However, on most other political questions, Potter and the other union leaders shared a common view and they collaborated in supporting campaigns for reforms at home as well as liberal causes abroad. With the development of the Trades Councils the unions had abandoned the non-political policy they had followed for the previous twenty-five years. This resurgence in political interest had been brought about by the steady growth of the unions, and the establishment of the national amalgamated trade societies, which were now anxious to have their status accepted and publicly recognised. As things stood, in the early 1860s, the unions were subject to serious legal restraints and their members were greatly discriminated against. How little the unions enjoyed the protection of the law was soon to be demonstrated by the Queen's Bench Division. Under the Master and Servant Law workers were treated as inferiors, they had little legal protection against dangerous working conditions, and as they had no vote they were denied the opportunity to bring about changes in the law by democratic means. It was only through the unions that they could hope to remedy this state of affairs and achieve what had been granted to the middle class by the Reform Act of 1832.

The idea of a national parliament of labour as a means of advancing the social and political interests of labour was advocated by the Operative Bricklayers' Society in 1861, but not taken up. In November of that year the Glasgow Trades Council called upon all the trade societies in the United Kingdom to embark on a campaign to achieve manhood suffrage, and to reform the law relating to master and servant and as it affected trade combinations. The London Trades Council refused to endorse the Glasgow suggestion, fearing that a political campaign might damage the unions, but a year later, it was prepared to support the establishment of a Manhood Suffrage and Vote by Ballot Association.

The Glasgow Trades Council continued to urge the trade societies to press for political changes and again took the initiative in calling a conference to secure national support from the trade societies for a campaign to achieve the amendment of the Master and Servant laws. Although the conference was small, most of the leading figures including Potter and members of the London Trades Council were present. The political campaign that followed proved to be a model of the kind of political pressure group activity that the trade unions were to use with great effect in the future. Members of Parliament were lobbied, meetings were organised and petitions in support of reform of the laws were presented. In 1865, a year after the campaign was launched, a Parliamentary Committee was appointed which reported in favour of a reform of the law and this was carried out in 1867. The Glasgow triumph had truly demonstrated what could be achieved by united action and a carefully mounted political campaign.

The trade union movement was unfortunately by no means united. The animosity between Potter and the leaders of the large trade unions had reached the point in 1865 when William Allan and his friends decided to secure his expulsion from the London Trades Council. The immediate cause of their anger was Potter's refusal to accept the advice of the London Trades Council, which claimed to speak on behalf of all trade societies, as the final word on the wisdom of taking strike action. Matters came to a head when Potter advised the striking North Staffordshire Iron Puddlers to ignore their own union executive and the London Trades Council, and to reject a proposal made by Lord Lichfield that they should return to work and accept arbitration. When Potter organised a series of meetings in support of the Iron Puddlers the Council was indignant. The President of the Amalgamated Society of Engineers denounced him as a 'strike jobber' and *The Beehive* 'his instrument for pushing his nose into every unfortunate dispute that sprang up'.

Shortly before he was voted out of the London Trades Council, Potter had been one of the main instigators of the National Reform League. This organisation was founded for the purpose of bringing together trade unionists and middle-class Radicals in a joint campaign to secure working men the vote. However, Potter soon came to the conclusion that the union leaders had allowed the National Reform League to become dominated by their middle-class Radical friends, who were not prepared to support the full manhood suffrage that Potter and his associates were demanding. Potter was in particular concerned that in the forthcoming Reform Bill provision should be made to entitle single men living in lodgings to vote. When he learned that the National Reform League was not prepared to press for such a clause in the Bill, he characteristically decided to set up his own organisation to lobby for the more radical Act that he favoured.

The new body was called the London Working Men's Association, a name which revived memories of the Chartist agitation for parliamentary reform of some thirty years earlier. The link with the earlier agitation was made actual by the appointment of an old Chartist, Robert Hartwell, Potter's collaborator on *The Beehive*, as secretary of the London Working Men's Association. The L.W.M.A. did not limit its activities to agitating for Parliamentary reform, and it was soon in dispute with the London Trades Council over the support that should be given to the Sheffield Association of Organised Trades, whose members employed in the file-making industry had been locked-out because they were demanding a wage increase. The lock-out was condemned by the London Trades Council, but when the Wolverhampton Trades Council urged that a conference of trade society delegates should be held in Sheffield to oppose the lock-out system, it was extremely reluctant to support the idea. Potter, however, immediately gave their resolution his enthusiastic backing and himself submitted a scheme for amalgamating the trade societies in every town in the kingdom into one great body with a responsible and ruling head; district labour parliaments would assemble quarterly and these district parliaments would then be represented in a national Labour Parliament which should meet annually.

The proposal of the Wolverhampton Trades Council was widely supported and the conference was duly held in Sheffield. This conference was one of the largest and most representative that had so far been held, but most of the delegates came from northern trades societies and councils. The leaders of the London Trades Council were represented solely by George Odger who attended for the purpose of exercising a watching brief rather than to give actual support. Potter was not able to be present, but the L.W.M.A. was represented and the leaders of the L.T.C. feared that the conference would be dominated by their hated rival and would adopt dangerously aggressive policies.

In the event, the delegates adopted a moderate and responsible attitude, but they demanded more positive and united action against lock-outs. It was decided to establish a permanent organisation which was given the name United Kingdom Alliance of Organised Trades. The aim of the Alliance was to build up a central fund from which aid could be given to societies whose members found themselves locked-out by employers. The Alliance was to be administered from Sheffield and William Dronfield, the secretary of the Sheffield Association of Organised Trades, was elected secretary. Dronfield, a journeyman compositor, was an exceptionally able trade unionist who was soon to play an important part in the founding of the T.U.C.

Unfortunately, there was a sharp growth in industrial unrest shortly after the Alliance was established and the Executive found itself unable to meet all the demands on the very limited resources of a newly created body. Support for the Alliance soon proved fickle and in the absence of help and assistance from the big unions there was little likelihood of its survival. The factor that really destroyed the Alliance, however, was the sudden revelation that some members of the Sheffield Trade Societies had resorted to intimidation and violence against workers who were unwilling to support militant policies.

3. A ROYAL COMMISSION ON TRADE UNIONS

The impact of the 'Sheffield outrages' on public opinion was such as to convince the leaders of the great national amalgamated societies that everything must be done to dissociate the unions from the criminal activities of a small number of irresponsible men. The London Trades Council immediately sent one of its senior members to investigate and report. It also called for a Commission of Enquiry, confident that the great body of trade unionists would be exonerated from any connection with the vicious activities that had been brought to light. Unfortunately for the Sheffield based Alliance it was discovered that treasurer William Broadhead was one of the ringleaders. This exposure inevitably led to press criticism of the Alliance and the withdrawal of support by many societies, even though the Alliance had been in no way responsible for the 'outrages'.

On 16 January 1867 the Court of the Queen's Bench added to the troubles of the trade unions by a decision which exposed their precarious legal status and left their funds without legal protection. The decision arose in connection with an action brought by the Boilermakers' Society against the treasurer of its Bradford branch who had wrongfully appropriated a sum of £24 belonging to the union. Up to this decision, unions had thought that they could take action against officials who embezzled union funds under the 1855 Friendly Societies Act, so long as they deposited their rules with the Registrar of Friendly Societes. The Court now held that the unions were not covered by this Act. The difficulty facing the unions lay in the fact that though repeal of the Combination Acts had made it lawful for workmen to act in combination to secure improvements in wages and hours of work, trade unions had not been given any corporate legal status. They were, in effect, no longer criminal organisations, but their activities, insofar as they were in restraint of trade, were illegal under the common law. Thus, if the unions were to be rescued from the predicament into which they had been placed by the Court's decision, it was necessary for Parliament to legislate in their favour. The prospects looked none too good when a few weeks after the Boiler-makers' Society decision the Government announced that it intended to appoint a Royal Commission to inquire into trade unions.

The unions realised at once that this decision was of vital significance. They had everything to gain and lose from the Commission's report and they acted at once to ensure that the unions' case would be put as vigorously and effectively as possible. To make certain that there would be no interference from Potter and his friends Allan and Applegarth and their associates decided to establish what they chose to call a 'Conference of Amalgamated Trades.' The object of the Conference was the creation of a standing body of senior trade union leaders who were able to meet regularly and at the shortest possible notice. Since the Conference was not an elected body, it was not bound to seek the support of any of the unions for whatever it might do. This self-appointed leadership of the trade union movement inevitably aroused a considerable distrust, especially among the provincial societies and trades councils who were inclined to follow the leadership of George Potter. The members of the Conference of Amalgamated Trades were looked upon by Potter as a clique and he often described them in *The Beehive* as the 'dirty pack'.

As soon as the Royal Commission was announced, Potter led a deputation from the London Working Men's Association to the Home Secretary to plead for the appointment of a working man on the Commission, or if the Government would not agree to that, one of the group of middle-class radicals who had proved to be staunch friends of the unions. The Home Secretary informed the deputation that he was appointing to the Commission Thomas Hughes and Lord Lichfield, who were well-known trade-union sympathisers. He also said that whilst the Government would not appoint a trade-union leader it would be prepared to appoint Frederic Harrison, a member of a small group of so-called positivists, who had been a frequent contributor to *The Beehive*.

One week later, the Conference of Amalgamated Trades sent a deputation to try to persuade the Home Secretary to appoint one of their number to the Commission. They failed to persuade the

Government to take this course, but it was agreed that the Conference of Amalgamated Trades should be allowed to have a representative in attendance at all the proceedings of the Commission.

The L.W.M.A. had taken steps to organise a national conference to be held in London on 5 March at the St. Martin's Hall, to discuss the decision of the Queen's Bench. This meeting was boycotted by the leaders of London Trades Council but it proved to be the most representative gathering of trade society delegates ever held. Most of the major provincial trade societies and trades councils sent representatives. Efforts were made to heal the breach between the Conference of Amalgamated Trades and Potter and his supporters. When, however, the representatives of the provincial trades societies, who had been invited to the L.W.M.A. sponsored gathering, met with the members of the Conference of Amalgamated Trades, they were told by William Allan that he and his associates would have nothing to do with Potter and his friends, whom he described as 'meddlers'.

A committee appointed at the St. Martin's Hall Conference organised by Potter now sought and was granted the same facility to have a representative at the sessions of the Royal Commission as had been given to the Conference of Amalgamated Trades. However, when the representative of Potter's Conference, Thomas Connolly, president of the Operative Stonemasons, made an indiscreet criticism to a trade-union gathering, of J. A. Roebuck, one of the Commissioners, the Commission refused henceforth to admit him to its proceedings. This step was taken with the support of the Conference of Amalgamated Trades which was only too ready to seize the first opportunity to get rid of its hated rivals. The Conference of Amalgamated Trades was thus left alone to organise the defence of the unions before the Commission. The collaboration between Robert Applegarth, Secretary of the Amalgamated Society of Carpenters and Joiners, who had been selected by the Conference of Amalgamated Trades for this task, and Frederic Harrison, Thomas Hughes and Lord Lichfield proved to be remarkably harmonious and effective, insofar as it led to the production of a powerful minority report that subsequently had great influence on the Government and the future system of industrial relations in Britain.

Effective as the work of Applegarth was, this could not be seen by those outside of the Conference of Amalgamated Trades. In September 1867 the London Trades Council and the Conference of Amalgamated Trades presented a report of the steps that they had taken to put the unions' case to the Royal Commission, but this did not allay a growing demand for a national conference and positive national leadership. However, the Conference of Amalgamated Trades had no wish to encourage outside interference and it was extremely reluctant to call a national conference before the Commission had reported. Potter and his followers were not satisfied with this situation and were determined to bring pressure to bear on the Conference of Amalgamated Trades, which they believed was prepared to settle for a revision of the law which would give the unions much less protection than they wished to obtain. They were in conflict with the Conference of Amalgamated Trades in particular over the extent to which the law should protect the right to strike. The Conference of Amalgamated Trades had given the impression that it would be satisfied with obtaining the full right to combine, protection for friendly society and other unions' funds, and the legal right of unions to invest their funds as they might choose. In the course of 1867, however, it became obvious even to the Conference of Amalgamated Trades that it was necessary to go beyond these limits and to seek legislation that would give the unions complete protection against actions under the law of conspiracy as well as protection for their funds.

While the Conference of Amalgamated Trades was edging gingerly towards the position already adopted by Potter and his supporters, pressure was growing for a national conference of trade societies. A year had elapsed since the St. Martin's Hall conference and in that time a good deal had happened. The long awaited Reform Bill had been passed and urban workers now had the right to vote, a right which it was clear they would soon be able to exercise for the first time. The London Working Men's Association was anxious that the unions should be ready to take advantage of the political opportunities that Parliamentary Reform offered. The Royal Commission was almost at the end of its labour and its report was expected in the relatively near future. Thus, the time seemed ripe for the sounding of union opinion and the consideration of policies and organisation for the future.

4. PROPOSALS FOR A CONGRESS

Chafing at the inactivity of the Conference of Amalgamated Trades, and by now anxious to bring the feud between himself and the Conference to an end, in part because he had come to recognise that only a united trade-union movement was likely to secure the kind of legislation that he desired, Potter took the initiative to end the quarrel. There was also another reason for this move; a financial one. *The Beehive* was in difficulties and if it was to be saved it would require the support of the large national amalgamated societies, which were the only source of the funds that were needed.

Potter's first proposal to the Conference of Amalgamated Trades was a scheme for a meeting between twelve representatives selected by the leading trade societies and twelve representatives of the employers who would together try to arrive at a national agreement to put an end to strikes and lock-outs. Allan and Applegarth and their friends would not have anything to do with the idea, suspecting that it had been promoted mainly for Potter's advantage, since it would clearly have involved the winding up of the Conference of Amalgamated Trades.

At the same time as Potter put forward this proposal the London Working Men's Association suggested that a 'National Parliament of Labour' should be held in London during May. When the L.W.M.A. made this suggestion Potter and his friends were not aware that two weeks earlier the Manchester and Salford Trades Council had made a similar proposal to hold a national trades' congress in Manchester in May. When Potter learned of the Manchester proposal he decided to counsel the L.W.M.A. to drop its idea in favour of supporting the northern gathering.

The Manchester and Salford Trades Council were seeking to establish a regular annual meeting along the lines of the Congress of the National Association for the Promotion of Social Science. This body had given some attention to trade societies and their activities and had published a report on *Trade Societies and Strikes* in 1860. It had also invited from time to time one or two leading trade union officers. In 1865 William Dronfield, secretary of the Sheffield Trades Council and of the ill-fated Sheffield based United Kingdom Alliance of Organised Trades, had been invited to read a paper on Trade Unions. This paper followed one by an arch-opponent of the unions which had been severely critical of their activities. Much to Dronfield's annoyance, when the official proceedings were published he found that his paper, which had defended the unions, had been omitted. Believing that a middle-class body would never give the union case a fair treatment Dronfield concluded that the unions ought to take their own steps to explain themselves to the public. Dronfield put this view to S. C. Nicholson and W. H. Wood, president and secretary of the Manchester and Salford Trades Council. They were convinced by Dronfield that it was time the unions had a congress of their own and they decided to take the initiative to realise this objective. Had the Conference of Amalgamated Trades not been a self-appointed, cliquish and autocratic body, it would have been the natural point of development for a national organisation of this kind. As it was, the Conference was recognised as doing a good job with regard to the Royal Commission, but it did not inspire enough confidence to be accepted as a permanent organisation representing all the unions.

5. THE MANCHESTER TRADES UNION CONGRESS

The Congress was planned to be held in Manchester on 4 May and to last not longer than six days. However, the organisers found that this date would not give the trade organisations invited enough time to select delegates or for the delegates time to prepare their papers. It was, therefore, decided to postpone the gathering until Whitsuntide.

Support for the Congress was almost certainly disappointing for the organisers, since only thirty-four delegates were present on 2 June at the Mechanics Institute, when the Congress was declared open. The delegates were mainly from provincial trades councils and northern trade societies. Potter and a representative of a small printing union were the only metropolitan delegates. The Conference of Amalgamated Trades and the London Trades Council ignored the Congress, regarding it as a potentially hostile body, especially since it was supported by Potter. Samuel Nicholson, the president of the Manchester and Salford Trades Council, was to have presided, but he had to attend the annual meeting of a friendly society of which he was general secretary. In his absence the delegates elected his colleague, W. H. Wood, secretary of the Manchester and Salford Trades Council, as President.

The procedure of the Congress was modelled on that of the Social Science Association, with papers on the following subjects being read and discussed:

1. Trade Unions an Absolute Necessity.
2. Trade Unions and Political Economy
3. The Effects of Trade Unions on Foreign Competition
4. Regulation of the Hours of Labour
5. Limitation of Apprentices
6. Technical Education
7. Courts of Arbitration and Conciliation
8. Co-operation
9. The Present Inequality of the Law in regard to Conspiracy, Picketing, Coercion, etc.
10. Factory Acts Extension Bill, 1867
11. The Legislation of Trade Societies
12. The Present Royal Commission on Trade Unions
13. The necessity of an Annual Congress of Trade Representatives from the Various Centres of Industry

Most of the papers were well prepared and the discussions that followed were usually sharply focused on the positive steps that might be taken to remedy the situation under discussion. This was no academic gathering content merely to raise issues and discuss theoretical solutions. The delegates were entirely concerned with achieving practical results. The desire to create an effective national organisation was made clear when a resolution was carried which held that 'it was highly desirable that the trades of the United Kingdom should hold an annual congress for the purpose of bringing the trades into closer alliance and to take action in all parliamentary matters pertaining to the general interests of the working classes'.

Although the delegates had fundamentally changed the concept of the Congress from the notion of a working-class social science association, set forth in the circular of invitation, Potter and his friends felt that they had not gone far enough. In Potter's view the time had arrived when it was necessary to bring all the trade societies together 'in a federated system something similar to that now in existence in North America'. This proposal harked back to the one big union idea which had been urged by Doherty and Owen. It was to come up again and again in the future and eventually to be tried, but in the hundred years that followed the first meeting, it was never to be accepted as an alternative to the concept of a Congress of autonomous trade unions concerned with bringing pressure to bear on governments to advance their common interests. The function of collective bargaining and fighting the employers was one primarily for the separate unions; in the opinion of most unions industrial negotiation was not a role for which a central association was best suited.

Before the Congress concluded it was agreed that the next should be held in Birmingham, and organised by the Birmingham Trades Council with the assistance of a committee of five which was elected by the Congress before it dispersed.

2 Consolidation and the Lib-Lab Alliance, 1868-94

I. ESTABLISHING THE LEGAL FRAMEWORK

THE first Trades Union Congress had undoubtedly been a considerable success, but George Howell, who was to become Secretary, stated over twenty years later, 'it was hardly expected even by the most sanguine of the promoters of the gathering that the one then being held would really constitute the first of a continuous series, though that was the dream and the hope of the originators of the movement.'[1]

Before the next Congress was held the eagerly awaited general election on the new register had taken place. Scant attention was given to the election by the Conference of Amalgamated Trades, but the London Working Men's Association under Potter's leadership worked hard to ensure that the newly enfranchised workers were on the electoral roll, and did what it could to help trade union candidates obtain nomination as Liberals. However, only two trade unionists and a well known co-operator eventually fought the election and all of them were defeated.

Some weeks prior to the election Peter Shorrocks, who had acted as secretary to the first Trades Union Congress, had called upon the trades societies that had supported the Congress to do everything in their power to put up trade unionists for election. Unfortunately the organisation to make this possible was completely lacking. The plain fact was that the trade unions had not yet realised the opportunity which the enfranchisement of the urban workers had provided. One of the few to realise the significance of the Reform Act was George Potter, whose newspaper, *The Beehive*, drew the moral from the failure to elect a single working man to Parliament that they should take steps to be better prepared next time.

With the Liberal victory and Gladstone, who was looked upon as a friend of the trade unions, as the Prime Minister, union

[1] G. Howell, 'Trades Union Congresses and Social Legislation', *Contemporary Review* (Sep. 1889) p. 405.

leaders hoped for the early appearance of a Trade Union Bill. The Royal Commission had not yet reported, but it was soon expected to do so. Before the election the London Working Men's Association had approached the Conference of Amalgamated Trades and the London Trades Council with the suggestion that a joint meeting should be held in support of a privately drafted Bill that would free the unions from the inimical effects of recent judicial decisions. The Conference of Amalgamated Trades, with hesitation and then reluctantly, finally agreed to the proposal. There was some difference of opinion between the sponsors of the Bill and a number of trade society delegates who felt that on the question of violence and intimidation the Bill conceded too much to the critics of trade unionism. However, it was finally agreed that the Bill should go forward as it had been drafted.

The Royal Commission's Report eventually appeared in March 1869. The majority report was much less damaging to the trade unions than had been expected when the Commission was set up. This was a tribute to the work of the Conference of Amalgamated Trades. It was also due to the brilliant work of Lichfield, Hughes and Harrison. These three had had considerable influence on the majority, but could not persuade them to go as far as they themselves wished to go. They, therefore, produced their own minority report which was based upon a penetrating analysis of the role of the unions in a modern society. The minority report advanced a simple and persuasive thesis that urged the sweeping away of all discrimination against workpeople. They sought to keep the courts out of union affairs by advocating only a limited recognition of the legal status of unions. What they primarily wished to achieve was a situation where any act done by more than one person would not be a crime if the same act when done by a single person would not be a crime. Following up their minority report Frederic Harrison drafted a Bill which if carried would have put into practice all the ideas which he and his colleagues had advocated.

The Conference of Amalgamated Trades and Potter's London Working Men's Association, though retaining a certain degree of mutual suspicion, called a truce to organise a joint campaign in support of the urgently needed Trade Union Bill. But the Conference of Amalgamated Trades was not persuaded that it should be represented at the second Trades Union Congress, which was postponed from May until August because of the meetings in London in support of the Trade Union Bill. However, the London Trades Council did participate on this occasion, sending George Odger as its delegate. In all some 47 delegates assembled in Birmingham, an increase of only thirteen over the previous year, but they represented twice as many trade unionists as at the first meeting, and, even more important, they came from a wider and more influential range of organisations.

The second Congress was conducted on similar lines to the first with papers being presented on a variety of subjects. The main discussion, however, was on the Trade Union Bill; this revealed some difference of opinion, but not sufficiently deep to prevent common action. Before the Congress adjourned it was decided to levy each society an annual fee to cover the costs of holding the Congress. It was also agreed that the next meeting of the Congress would take place in London and be organised by the London Trades Council.

The choice of London as the next venue of the Trades Union Congress arose from the recognition by the delegates that the battle for the Trade Union Bill they desired to see become law was going to be fought in London. The leaders of the Congress were aware of the need to make common cause with the Conference of Amalgamated Trades, partly because they had no wish to leave this unrepresentative group to press the unions' case but also because they knew that if they were divided they would not be able to bring as strong pressure as they would if united. Selecting London, however, put the organisation of the next Congress into the hands of the London Trades Council, which in effect meant putting it under the influence of the Conference of Amalgamated Trades.

William Allan and Robert Applegarth looked upon the Trades Union Congress as an upstart body and there is no doubt that they did not accept the need for a central body of this kind. However, they saw the London meeting as a useful gathering to put pressure on the Government when the official Trade Union Bill was published. Since the Government's Bill had not appeared by the summer of 1870[1] the London Trades Council, under the influence of the Conference of Amalgamated Trades, decided to postpone the annual meeting until the next session of Parliament which

[1] The Government had passed a temporary Trade Union Funds Protection Act in 1869 as a stopgap measure while it made up its mind on the major issues.

would be convened at the beginning of 1871. This decision gave rise to much dissatisfaction and the minutes of the London Trades Council reveal that it was finally compelled to summon the Congress, which it did at very short notice in March 1871.

The publication of the Bill, which followed the principles laid down by Lichfield, Hughes and Harrison, promised to give the unions the freedom to carry out their normal activities without fear of litigation and criminal proceedings except in one very important respect. This was in respect of the conduct of strikes. The third clause of the Bill, which dealt with threats and the use of violence, intimidation, molestation, persistent following, watching and besetting, raised considerable apprehension. The unions were afraid that the courts would be able to interpret these crimes in such a way as to make any form of picketing during a strike impossible to carry out without committing an offence.

The advisers of the Conference of Amalgamated Trades were persuaded that the third clause was a price that unions must pay to secure the other freedoms that they desired. They believed, as did the majority of the Royal Commission, that the Sheffield outrages had shown that there was a danger that strong unions might use their power to coerce individuals by intimidatory methods. The members of the Conference of Amalgamated Trades were at first disposed to accept the opinions of their advisers and they may well not have opposed the 'third clause' had not Potter and his friends, who had seen this possibility for some time, aroused trade-union opinion against following this course.

When the third Congress finally opened, opposition to the 'third clause' was so strong that there was a demand that the whole Bill should be resisted unless the clause was amended or deleted. A deputation was sent to the Home Secretary to protest against this section of the Bill and Congress adjourned early each day so that members could go to the House of Commons to lobby Members of Parliament.

To ensure that pressure was kept up on the Government to secure the abolition of the 'third clause' and to press for the carrying out of its broader programme of legislation, the Congress elected a Parliamentary Committee that was empowered to co-operate with the London Trades Council and London trades societies. George Potter, who had now made his peace with the

Conference of Amalgamated Trades, and who had been elected President of the Congress, was elected chairman of the Parliamentary Committee. George Howell was elected secretary and Alexander Macdonald, Lloyd Jones and Joseph Leicester as members. Later on William Allan, who had been elected as treasurer to the Congress agreed to serve as treasurer of the Parliamentary Committee.

The Committee met immediately after the Congress and sent a strong letter, signed by Potter, Howell, Macdonald, Leicester and Jones, to every M.P. drawing their attention to the resolution passed by Congress, which refused to accept a Bill which 'presupposes criminal intentions or tendencies on the part of English workmen as a class'.[1] This letter and a deputation to the Home Secretary persuaded the Government to split the Bill into two parts. Thus the 'third clause' was taken out from the Trade Union Bill to become the Criminal Law Amendment Bill. This step did not satisfy the Parliamentary Committee, but it was to help the unions in the long run. The Conference of Amalgamated Trades considered that the Parliamentary Committee was adopting a policy that was too militant and protested that it had not been consulted by the Committee before it acted. George Howell smoothed things over, but the Committee had quite clearly established itself as the spokesman for the whole trade-union movement and the Conference of Amalgamated Trades had little choice but to accept this fact. They did so as soon as the two Bills became Acts of Parliament and from that time onwards the societies led by members of the Conference supported the Trades Union Congress.

The conflict between Potter and the Conference of Amalgamated Trades was over. Both had made very great contributions. Though they represented different elements and were often in fundamental disagreement they each represented essential features of the trade-union movement. Potter with his radical, aggressive, sometimes irresponsible ideas aroused great enthusiasm and a large following. Leader of a small society, more of a journalist and propagandist than a negotiator, he carried few administrative responsibilities. Allan and Applegarth, on the other hand, were the products of the large-scale unions. The national amalgamated societies were in many respects akin to big business organisations.

[1] Roberts, *The Trades Union Congress, 1868–1921.*

They had many thousands of members, massive resources, and provided an important social service through their friendly benefits that had to be carefully administered and guarded against policies that might undermine their stability. The leaders of large unions were prepared to call out their members on strike when this would serve a useful purpose, but they wanted above all to make trade unionism respectable so that it could exercise a powerful influence on national economic and social policy as an integrated element in the state rather than as a rebellious minority continuously engaged in militant protest.

The foundations of the T.U.C. had been put down, but they had still to be consolidated. This was largely achieved in the next few years. The fourth Trades Union Congress took further important steps forward in its organisation. The Social Science Association model had now been largely abandoned. What had emerged was a national association of trade unions whose function was to act as a union of the unions in negotiation with the Government in those matters on which it was necessary to legislate.

When the fourth Congress came to a close it had decided to ask its Parliamentary Committee to seek to secure the repeal of the Criminal Law Amendment Act; a Bill to improve safety in the mines; an abolition of the Truck Act; a Conciliation and Arbitration Act; and a Workmen's Compensation Act.

The Liberal Government was not disposed to try to repeal the Criminal Law Amendment Act, since it knew it would be unlikely to get the repeal through the House of Lords. When the next election came round in 1874 the Parliamentary Committee decided to make this a major issue of the campaign. Candidates of both parties were closely examined on their attitude to the Act and Disraeli indicated that if he were returned his party would amend the Act. How far this was a major factor in the victory that he secured is difficult to say, but the trade-union leaders did assume that he would be prepared at once to introduce a short amending Act. However, instead he set up a Royal Commission on Labour Laws and the Queen asked the two trade unionists who for the first time had been elected as Members of Parliament, to serve. The Parliamentary Committee was angry with Disraeli for engaging in what they saw as evasive tactics and they were even more annoyed when they discovered that he had invited Alexander Macdonald and Thomas Burt to be members. In the event Burt refused the invitation, but Macdonald accepted and produced a minority report calling for the repeal of the Criminal Law Amendment Act, a drastic change in the Master and Servant Law, and a revision of the law relating to conspiracy under which trade unionists were liable to be prosecuted when going on strike. The Royal Commission on Labour Laws had occasioned some delays, but the Conservative Government acted promptly after the Commission had reported.

Congress met twice in 1875, once in January and then again in October – which henceforth was to be the normal month of meeting – so as to prepare the legislative programme in advance of the new parliamentary session. When the second Congress of 1875 met, the Parliamentary Committee was able to report the passing of the Conspiracy and Protection of Property Act, which repealed the Criminal Law Amendment Act, redefined peaceful picketing and freed the unions from the taint of criminal conspiracy. Also an Employer and Workmen Act, which abolished the discriminatory aspects of the Master and Servant Law, and by its very name acknowledged a new era in industrial relations.

So delighted was George Howell, the secretary of the Parliamentary Committee, with these advances, he came to the conclusion that the Trades Union Congress had fulfilled its purpose and now might safely be wound up. He found fews upporters, except among the followers of the London Trades Council, whose leaders were anxious to carry out the functions of the Parliamentary Committee. Howell resigned and in his place Congress elected Henry Broadhurst, a leader of the Stonemasons' union and former associate of George Potter.

2. THE LIB-LAB ALLIANCE AND THE NEW UNIONISM

During the next fifteen years Broadhurst built up the T.U.C. into a powerful national organisation in close association with the Liberal Party. During those years British industry continued to expand, but the growth of the economy was interrupted by periods of severe depression. Up to this stage of their development the trade unions were mainly composed of skilled artisans; the growing numbers of labourers and less skilled workers, with the exception of those employed in the textile and mining industries and railways, were not organised. During the depressed years the more highly skilled workers were not hit quite as hard as the unskilled workers by the sharp rises in unemployment that occurred, and the unions, preoccupied with their own problems, showed relatively little concern for the plight of those who were not organised.

Outside of the unions there was a growing concern for the unemployed and the increasing awareness of the social problems of the 'lumpen proletariat' that existed in the rapidly expanding industrial cities began to stimulate new social and political ideas. Established modes of thought began to be questioned. Liberal economic doctrines came increasingly under attack. There were growing demands for state assistance, and socialism, thought of mainly as an alien European idea, began again to be advocated by advanced thinkers. The Social Democratic Federation, founded in 1881, adopted Marxism as its creed in 1883. In 1884 the Fabian Society was established to proclaim the virtues of the new doctrines of state and municipal socialism. The Fabians agreed with the Marxists that socialism was inevitable, but not by revolution; they believed that it would come by gradual evolution. Henry George attacked the established economic and social system from the same angle of the maldistribution of wealth and political power, but he found his panacea in a simple reform of the fiscal system. If all taxes were abolished and replaced by one single tax on land every economic and social problem could be solved; it was an attractively simple remedy that fooled no one but its advocates.

Up to 1886 there were few signs of the influence of the new forces on the T.U.C. and the unions. In that year Henry Broadhurst, who had earlier become a Lib-Lab member of Parliament, was appointed a junior minister in Mr. Gladstone's newly elected government. This was a reward for Broadhurst's loyal support of the Liberals, and confirmation of the official status that had been attained by the T.U.C. But Broadhurst was not in office long, since in 1886 the economic depression became almost as bad as it had been in 1879 and Gladstone was forced by his weak political position to resign. When Broadhurst returned to the T.U.C. after a mere nine months in Whitehall he found the first signs of discontent with the T.U.C.'s traditional support for the Liberals.

There was relatively little enthusiasm inside the unions for the new Socialist ideas, but it was evident that whatever the attitude of the Parliamentary Committee might be it was going to be difficult to keep the rising tempo of radicalism from influencing them. The 1886 Congress was held against a background of massive demonstrations of unemployed workers, led by two fiery young skilled engineers, John Burns and Tom Mann, in alliance with the Marxist leader of the S.D.F., H. M. Hyndman, and the leader of the Socialist League, William Morris. The President for that year focused the attention of the delegates on issues the Parliamentary Committee was not keen to have discussed, calling for a legal eight-hour day, nationalisation of the land and a vigorous onslaught on capitalism, but during the course of the week Broadhurst had little difficulty in diverting delegates away from taking the paths suggested by the President.

In the following year the situation was less easily handled. The President on this occasion was a Welshman named Bevan whose address was mainly devoted to attacking capitalism and calling for a vast programme of state intervention. He concluded, 'Gentlemen, socialism has lost its terrors for us. We recognise our most serious evils in the unrestrained, unscrupulous and remorseless forces of capitalism'. The President's theme was taken up with vigour by a new delegate to Congress from Ayrshire. Keir Hardie was at this stage a Liberal, but he was rapidly coming to the conclusion that only socialism could bring about a society in which wealth and power were shared more equally as he believed God had intended. Hardie saw in Broadhurst a man who was betraying the interests of the workers for the benefit of the social classes who enjoyed vast wealth and supreme political power. He was particularly angry because Broadhurst would not support a legal limit of eight hours work a day and because he supported well-to-do Liberal candidates instead of insisting that working-class men should be selected. Broadhurst had little difficulty in defending himself against this rather bitter personal attack, but he was unable to prevent the delegates from passing a resolution instructing the Parliamentary Committee to take a plebiscite of the members of the unions to find out whether a reduction of hours should be brought about by trade-union action or legislation.

At the next Congress Hardie returned to the attack, but without much success, against the solidly entrenched Broadhurst. However, 1889 brought a dramatic change. The trade union world had been astonished in 1888 by the sudden strike of girls employed at the

Bryant and May factory which had been organised by an outsider, Mrs. Annie Besant, who upbraided the unions for leaving it to her, 'a woman of the middle class', to organise these wretched, poorly paid, unskilled workers. The victory of the match girls gave a tremendous fillip to the organisation of the less skilled workers. Helped by a change in the economic climate which was now more favourable, with trade booming and unemployment falling sharply, John Burns, Tom Mann and Will Thorne set about organising a Gas Workers and General Labourers' union. The new union succeeded in securing a reduction in the working day of gas stokers from twelve hours to eight hours almost without a struggle. This swift success stimulated the dock labourers to join the union that Ben Tillett had organised in 1887. Sensing that the moment was right to make a general claim, Tillett called on every docker to support the demand for a basic rate of sixpence an hour. Within a few days thousands had joined the union and come out on strike. Burns and Mann joined Tillett and together they gave the dockers brilliant leadership that won public sympathy for their cause and finally compelled the port employers to concede practically the whole of the men's demands.

The upsurge of the new unions had an important impact on the T.U.C. At the 1890 Congress Keir Hardie was joined by Burns, Mann and Tillett who had become national figures. The critical moment arrived with the moving of the eight-hour-day motion, which had become the symbol of the struggle for power in the Congress between the old Lib-Lab leadership which favoured voluntary agreement and the new radical socialists, who wanted legislation. The resolution was carried, but only by a small majority. However, the representative of the Stonemasons, Broadhurst's own union, had dramatically informed the delegates that he had been instructed to support a legally imposed eight-hour maximum day.

At the end of the Congress John Burns boasted that the delegates had passed sixty resolutions of which forty-five asked for state or municipal interference on behalf of the weak against the strong.

Faced by the defeat of the policies for which Congress had long stood, Broadhurst decided to resign as secretary, giving ill-health as the reason. The main supporter of the Lib-Lab alliance was now out of the way, but the T.U.C. had by no means been completely captured by the socialists. Charles Fenwick, M.P., a Northumberland miner, the man who was elected in Broadhurst's place as secretary of the Parliamentary Committee, was an equally strong supporter of Gladstonian liberalism. Moreover, the new Parliamentary Committee was composed mainly of old unionists. John Burns managed to be elected, but he was bottom of the list and only secured a place on the Committee because the man above him, a Lib-Lab, decided not to serve after being elected.

The old unionists realised, however, that the socialists might soon be able to secure a majority on the Parliamentary Committee and they were determined to prevent this from happening if they could. Ironically they found their erstwhile critic, John Burns, joining with them to defeat his former associates, Tom Mann and Keir Hardie. Burns, who was not an ideological socialist, had developed a bitter hatred of Keir Hardie and a deep antipathy to the newly established Independent Labour Party. Beatrice Webb noted in her diary that Burns's dislike of Hardie amounted to a mania.

In 1894 Burns, together with James Mawdsley, a leader of the Cotton Spinners, who was a strong supporter of the Conservative Party, seized the opportunity, when the Congress remitted a number of resolutions calling for changes in the Standing Orders, to revise the constitution of the T.U.C. so as to prevent the socialists from gaining control.[1] The Parliamentary Committee on the casting vote of its chairman, David Holmes, a leader of the Cotton Weavers and a firm believer in the Lib-Lab alliance, decided to limit the membership of the Congress to trade societies only; to restrict delegates to men who were either working at their trade or were full time paid officials of their unions; and to institute a system of block voting which would give the big unions the dominant position at Congress.

There was an element of ambiguity in the resolution remitting the motions to the Parliamentary Committee concerning when any changes should come into force, which gave Burns and his colleagues the opportunity to put the changes into effect as soon as they were adopted by the Parliamentary Committee; they then announced that the new rules would apply to the next Congress, although they had not been voted on by the affiliated societies.

An attempt was made at the next Congress to censure the

[1] For a full account of this affair see Roberts, *The Trades Union Congress, 1868-1921*, pp. 143 *et seq.*

B

Parliamentary Committee for acting contrary to the constitution of the T.U.C., but this was overwhelmingly defeated under the new voting system; the coal and cotton unions which had together the largest block of votes, as expected, supported the Committee.

The factor which had finally persuaded Burns and Mawdsley to act as they had done was the establishment of the Independent Labour Party in 1893 under Hardie's leadership. The I.L.P. had strong support in the Trades Councils and it was feared that it might gain control of the Congress through these bodies. Although the Trades Councils had been responsible for founding the T.U.C. it was now argued that their affiliation was anomalous and simply amounted to dual representation.

The change relating to the qualification of delegates was calculated to get rid of Keir Hardie, who was no longer working as a miner, but as a journalist and lecturer. The block voting system could be justified as a genuine extension of democracy and a legitimate change since it enabled voting at Congress to reflect more fairly the distribution of the membership. But undoubtedly the main reason for the change was to keep Socialists off the Parliamentary Committee and to secure the defeat of Socialist resolutions.

The representatives of the Trades Councils who had attended the 1895 Congress in the hope that they would be admitted considered establishing a rival organisation – as in fact they eventually did in Scotland – but they were warned by Tom Mann and Ben Tillett that this would be a mistake. Summing up the situation three weeks after the Congress Mann wrote:

It is an altogether mistaken view to suppose that by narrowing the basis of representation at the Congress, that therefore, either Socialism or Socialists will be kept out. Both the cause and the men will continue to make themselves felt. . . . Some think that it's a case of skilled men who are anti-socialist, and the unskilled who are Socialists. This is not so. The position in which the miners' delegates found themselves when considering the Collectivist resolution is indicative of what may be expected from all the large unions at an early date, viz. as many for Socialism as against it.[1]

[1] *Labour Leader* (28 Sep 1895).

3 The Emergence of the Labour Movement, 1894-1914

I. THE ENGINEERING LOCK-OUT AND THE GENERAL FEDERATION OF TRADE UNIONS

SHORTLY before the Trades Union Congress accepted the new standing orders the Liberal Government was defeated and the Conservatives returned to office to remain in power for ten years. During their first year the new Government carried out a recommendation of the Royal Commission on Labour, which had reported in 1894, by passing a Conciliation Act. This Act gave the Labour Department of the Board of Trade power to encourage the formation of voluntary Joint Conciliation Boards and to use its 'good offices' to bring the parties in a dispute together, and to appoint conciliators and arbitrators at the request of the parties. The Act brought the State into the settlement of disputes, but without giving it any power to impose terms on either party.

There was need for some positive action along these lines since industrial relations had been steadily deteriorating during the previous few years. Conflict between unions and employers was growing more acute as employers sought to reinstate their authority and to curb the expansion of the unions. One of the factors which had greatly embittered relations had been the establishment in 1893 of a National Free Labour Association by a former trade unionist named William Collison. The object of the Association was to undermine the power of the unions by providing 'blacklegs' when required by employers through so-called Free Labour Registries. The resort to blackleg labour during industrial disputes aroused great indignation and on a number of occasions violence was provoked.

The employers sought to protect their interests by setting up an association which it was believed would have the strength to stand up to the nationally organised trade unions. The Engineering Employers' Federation, which was established in 1896, was determined to make it possible for its members to manage their firms in an efficient way without interference from the unions. The issue between the Engineering Employers' Federation and the Amalgamated Society of Engineers came to a head on a demand that the daily hours of work should be reduced to eight without any loss of pay. A number of firms had already agreed to these terms, but when the A.S.E. called a strike against those firms that would not reduce their hours to eight a day, the E.E.F. called on its members to lock-out 25 per cent of the men employed in engineering throughout the country. The dispute rapidly escalated into a general stoppage of great national significance and it soon became clear that what was at stake was something more important than the eight-hour day.

It was a time of rapid technological change and the skilled unions in most industries had resisted the introduction of labour-saving machinery which they feared would result in redundancy and the replacement of skilled by unskilled workers. Here was the centre of the conflict. Management believed that its power to manage was being steadily eroded by trade union refusal to accept new methods and that it was essential to reassert managerial prerogatives.

It was quickly recognised by both sides that the eight-hour-day dispute had become a conflict of fundamental principles. As a condition of lifting the lock-out the engineering employers insisted on the workers accepting overtime as and when required by the employer; piece-rated wages; the abolition of restrictive appren-ticeship rules and an acknowledgment by the union that it had no right to bargain for apprentices. Faced by this challenge the A.S.E. was determined not to concede the terms demanded by the E.E.F. The lock-out lasted from July 1897 to January 1898. By that time both sides were feeling the strain and the strike and lock-out was called off with the financially severely strained union conceding most, but not all, of the employers' demands.

The effect of the engineering lock-out on the trade-union world was considerable. It convinced many trade unionists that it was imperative to develop a central trade union federation that would enable the unions to render mutual assistance through a central strike and lock-out fund and so be able to bolster up a union finding itself in the position of the A.S.E. The question had been raised at the T.U.C. on a number of occasions from its earliest days, but nothing had come of the resolutions passed. Under the influence of the 1897 lock-out the Congress decided to establish a committee to examine 'the best means of federating the trade unions'.

This Committee reported favourably to the 1898 Congress, which instructed the Parliamentary Committee to call a special conference by the following January. Like the first T.U.C. this conference was held in Manchester. At the conference a General Federation of Trade Unions was established, but it was not quite the organisation its founders had hoped to create. In the first place only forty-four societies, with about a quarter of the total membership of the unions, affiliated to the G.F.T.U. In the second place the rules gave far less power to the Management Committee than the sponsors thought desirable. The fact was the large unions were not willing to give up their sovereign powers and this had to be recognised for there to be any hope of attracting their support. But perhaps of even greater significance was the realisation that the mutual insurance fund would rapidly be dissipated if member organisations were constantly involved in strikes and lock-outs. The Federation had then from the outset to discourage militancy and seek for peaceful settlements rather than to promote aggressive action. Ironically, the factor that probably contributed most to the survival of the Federation during the initial period was a series of legal decisions culminating in the Taff Vale judgment that made striking extremely hazardous and reduced the calls on the insurance funds.

2. A LABOUR PARTY ESTABLISHED

The threat to the unions from the offensive mounted by the employers, the unfavourable decisions of Courts, together with resentment at the refusal of the Conservative Government to come to grips with any of the great social questions and the apparent weakness of the Liberal opposition, produced a growing conviction that it was necessary to secure a substantial increase in the number of Labour representatives in Parliament. With a general election in the offing, the supporters of the establishment of a trade union sponsored Labour Party were able to persuade the delegates to the 1899 Congress to pass a resolution by 546,000 votes to 434,000 instructing the Parliamentary Committee to summon a conference in co-operation with co-operative and socialistic working class organisations, 'to devise ways and means for securing the return of an increased number of Labour members to Parliament'.

After a good deal of manœuvring the conference was duly held at the Memorial Hall, Farringdon Street, on 17 February 1900. Fortunately for those who wished to see the establishment of a Labour Party, most of the strongest opponents did not bother to attend. The Conference eventually endorsed a plan to establish 'a distinct Labour Group in Parliament who shall have their own whips, and agree upon their policy'; and set up a Labour Representation Committee consisting of seven trade unionists, two members of the I.L.P., two S.D.F. and one Fabian. The duty of the Committee was to prepare a list of candidates, administer funds, to convene an annual conference and to keep in touch with the trade unions. During the first few years there was some ambiguity as to the exact relationship between the T.U.C. and the Labour Representation Committee. The situation was made clear when the President of the T.U.C. declared that the delegates had no power to 'endorse or amend the constitution of an independent and outside body'. Ramsay MacDonald, speaking as the fraternal delegate from the L.R.C. sought to allay fears by stating that the L.R.C. was the child of the Congress and they had come to offer their filial respects. With three separate national organisations in existence it was inevitable that problems of co-ordination and common policy would arise. To consider how the danger of conflict could be reduced, a meeting of representatives of the T.U.C., G.F.T.U. and the L.R.C. was arranged at the Caxton Hall, London. At this meeting an agreement was reached to set up a Joint Board as a permanent co-ordinating committee. It was also agreed at this meeting that in the forthcoming general election all candidates approved by the Parliamentary Committee and the L.R.C. would receive the full support of both organisations. There were still a large number of Lib-Lab Members of Parliament and the unions supporting these members had no intention of withdrawing their support in the forthcoming election.

During 1905 the T.U.C. adopted its own election programme of legislative action and called upon Trades Councils throughout the country to organise conferences and public meetings in support. The L.R.C. also issued its own manifesto which followed fairly closely the one put out by the T.U.C. The Parliamentary Committee endorsed fifty-one Labour candidates, of whom fifteen were

not supported by the L.R.C., mainly because they were representatives of the miners who still remained aloof. A number of
older Lib-Labs, including Thomas Burt, John Burns, W. Randal
Cremer, Charles Fenwick and Henry Broadhurst received no
endorsement from either the T.U.C. or the L.R.C.

The election was fought mainly on the question of tariff
protection; Home Rule for Ireland and a Trade Dispute Bill to
reverse the Taff Vale decision. The result was a tremendous
victory for the Liberal-Labour Alliance. The Liberals, together
with Labour, had the colossal majority of 271 over the Conservatives and their supporters. The L.R.C. now found that it had
twenty-nine Members of Parliament in its ranks. In addition,
twenty-five Lib-Labs had been elected. This astonishing result
had been produced mainly by Ramsay MacDonald's secret
agreement with Herbert Gladstone to permit L.R.C. candidates
in a number of seats to run without Liberal opposition. On the
morrow of the election, the L.R.C. announced that henceforth it
would be called the Labour Party and would have its own officers
and whips.

No fewer than nine out of the thirteen members of the Parliamentary Committee had been elected, six of them under the L.R.C.
banner and three as Lib-Labs. The influence of this Parliamentary
Committee group was considerable, and it helped to bring the
Lib-Lab and the Labour Party members together so that by the
end of that Parliament there was no longer any strong union
opposition to the Labour Party.

The report of the Royal Commission on Trade Disputes, which
had been appointed by the Government in 1903 to consider the
effect of the Taff Vale decision, was published during the general
election, but its report gave little satisfaction to the unions. The
Commission proposed that the unions should be declared corporate
associations by statute, but that they should be liable for the actions
of their members only if these had been expressly authorised by an
executive committee. In addition, the agreements entered into by
unions with employers or with their own members would be legally
binding and enforceable through the Courts. Strikes, whether
primary or secondary, whatever the motive behind them, should be
declared lawful, unless criminal or in breach of contract. The union
would then be liable to be sued for damages if it deliberately broke
a contract; the Commission therefore suggested that the benefit

funds should be separated from the general funds and be immune from any damages that might be granted against a union. There were a number of other recommendations giving union officers and members further legal protection.

The Parliamentary Committee issued a statement soon after the Report appeared, stating that it refused to accept the Commission's findings. The Government, under an obligation to produce a Trades Dispute Bill, acted quickly, but the result did not please the T.U.C., since the Bill followed the lines of the Royal Commission's report. When, however, it became clear that during the election most Liberal and Labour members had pledged their support for the T.U.C. draft Bill, which was designed to give the trade unions complete immunity from any action in the Courts, the Government abandoned its own measure to give the unions the Act they wanted.

In the next few years the Liberal Government carried out most of the programme of legislation that had been canvassed by the T.U.C. during the election. In addition to the Trades Disputes Act, the Government also passed, in its first year of office, the second point on the T.U.C.'s election programme. This was an important change in the law which gave an additional six million workers compensation for injury at work; the Act also extended the law to cover a schedule of six industrial diseases – this number was increased to twenty-four in the following year.

The Government was reluctant to concede the T.U.C.'s demand for a general eight-hours act, but it decided after some delay to satisfy the Lib-Lab miners by passing an Act limiting hours of work in the coal mines to eight a day.

Soon after the Government took office the Parliamentary Committee asked the Government to introduce a system of old age pensions. At the 1907 Congress a resolution was passed, criticising the Government for delay in making this reform and calling for revisions in fiscal policy that would make it possible for a state pension to be paid to all persons aged sixty and over. This was followed by a series of large meetings in all the main industrial centres. A Pensions Bill was introduced in 1908 by Lloyd George, the Chancellor of the Exchequer, and the Act came into force on 1 January 1909.

In 1909 the Government carried state intervention a stage further with the passing of the Trade Boards Act. This Act enabled Trade Boards to be established for so-called sweated industries, with power to propose minimum levels of pay that were legally binding upon the employers. The Parliamentary Committee had been instructed to support the Sweated Industries Bill sponsored by the Labour Party, but the Committee was not greatly enthusiastic about this measure. There seems to have been a good deal of scepticism as to the wisdom of the Trade Board concept and the establishment of legal minimum wages. Many trade unionists feared that these might become maximums and that the Trade Boards might detract from the merits of collective bargaining. A less respectable reason for the lack of interest was the fact that the Trade Boards mainly covered women workers, few of whom were in trade unions.

The trade unions were more interested in other measures concerning the establishment of employment exchanges and a system of unemployment and sickness insurance. As soon as the Parliamentary Committee discovered it was the Government's intention to legislate on these matters after the Royal Commission on the Poor Law had reported, probably on the lines already followed in Germany, it decided to send a delegation to investigate the German scheme. On its return, the delegation reported favourably on employment exchanges and more cautiously on unemployment and sickness insurance. Soon afterwards, Winston Churchill, President of the Board of Trade, introduced a Bill to establish Labour Exchanges. Some trade unionists were afraid that labour exchanges might be used, as the voluntary ones had been used in the 1890s, to supply blackleg labour during a strike. To meet these fears Churchill established a commission consisting of an employer, a trade-union leader and a civil service commissioner to appoint all the senior officials who would be concerned with the administration of the labour exchanges. He also invited the Parliamentary Committee to act as a sub-committee which would be consulted by him whenever advice was required on the running of the new employment service. These were important developments in the status of the trade-union movement.

The relation of the trade unions to the state was extended in another direction when the Government decided to introduce a system of unemployment and sickness insurance. This decision was welcomed by the T.U.C. and the G.F.T.U. since it offered the trade unions opportunity to participate in the administration of the scheme. Socialists who were against the insurance principle were much opposed to the Government's proposals and when the issue was debated at the Congress they supported the Minority Report of the Royal Commission on the Poor Law prepared by Beatrice Webb. The Minority Report, which favoured a state financed scheme, had been signed by the trade union represent- ative on the Commission. It was now repudiated by the Parlia- mentary Committee, whose views were upheld by a majority of the delegates.

3. THE SYNDICALIST REVOLT

During the five years in which it had been in power the Liberal Government had laid the basis for the modern welfare state. The tremendous steps forward which it had taken had been accom- panied, however, by growing social conflict and an upsurge of militancy which produced one of the greatest outbreaks of indus- trial unrest that had ever been known in Britain.

The underlying factor in this strike wave was undoubtedly economic. Although the old, the sick and the unemployed were all better protected than ever before, the young, able-bodied workers were less well off since prices had been rising since 1896 and as a result real wages actually fell between 1900 and 1910. Unemployment was high in 1907, 1908 and 1909, but it went down sharply thereafter. With returning prosperity workers felt that this was an opportunity to win back the loss that they had suffered in real wages.

Important as the economic factors were, they were not the only ones influencing the behaviour of the workers. Other elements in society at higher social levels were also showing that when they felt they had sufficient justification they were prepared to defy the law and established conventions of behaviour. The House of Lords, the suffragettes and the officers of the Army in Ireland all demonstrated that they were prepared to take things into their own hands in order to achieve their own political goals. Thus the unions were encouraged to use militant tactics.

The strike wave actually began in 1908; it fell back a little in 1909, but welled up again in 1910 and following years until checked by the outbreak of war in 1914.

Deeply involved in many of the strikes that broke out at this time was the former associate of John Burns and Ben Tillett, Tom Mann. Tom Mann had left Britain in 1902, dissatisfied with progress towards socialism, to settle in Australia, where Labour governments had been in power in various states for some time. However, Tom Mann had been unimpressed by the social legislation of Australia and New Zealand and had developed a deep distrust of Labour politicians and the bureaucratic state. He had, in fact, become a convert to syndicalism. Eventually, he decided to come back to Britain to preach his new faith.

On his return, Mann began to propagate his ideas through a series of pamphlets issued under the title of the *Industrial Syndicalist*. Mann found a sympathetic audience for his syndicalist message among young workers who felt that the Labour Party had simply become a subordinate section of the Liberal Party, and that the leadership of the unions was senile, weak and ineffective.

Tom Mann attacked the unions as moribund. They were unable to challenge the capitalist bosses effectively because they had adopted the philosophy of capitalism. They sought to advance the sectional interest of their members without regard to those workers who were in a weak bargaining position. He advocated the destruction of craft unions and in their place the establishment of industrial unions linked together through national federations under the central direction of the General Federation of Trade Unions. He urged the abandonment of the established pattern of collective bargaining and system of agreements, because it bolstered the existing structure of ownership and management. In Mann's eyes, a collective agreement bound the worker to an immoral system which ought to be destroyed. The most effective way of achieving its destruction was through strikes. Industrial conflict would eventually lead to the revolutionary strike which would result in the downfall of the capitalist state. At this stage the workers, through the reorganized unions, would take over the task of running the state and managing industry directly.

How many trade unionists Tom Mann converted to belief in industrial syndicalism it is impossible to say, but his doctrines certainly had a strong appeal to the workers of South Wales and the Clyde valley, and especially to the miners in these areas. Whether the doctrine was accepted or not, there was a ready ear for his advocacy of direct action, particularly in those industries such as mining, docks and railways where the management had long ruled autocratically, often refusing to negotiate issues in dispute with the unions.

In 1910 and 1911 many of the strikes that occurred, although they were often called by local leaders against the advice of the union, proved successful. The employers then inevitably recovered their wind and decided to stand firm and to make fewer concessions in the future. In 1912 the storm centre was again the coal fields; the miners were insisting upon the establishment of a minimum wage, but the owners refused to concede this demand. More than a million men in the coal industry came out on strike in 1912 on this issue. Having failed to persuade the owners and the miners to agree on settlement, the Government decided to introduce a national minimum wage Bill for the mining industry, which would guarantee a miner working in an abnormal place a minimum wage fixed by a District Board. When the Act became law, it was reluctantly accepted by the owners, but when put to a ballot vote of the miners it was rejected. The majority against was, however, regarded by the miners' leaders as too narrow to justify continuance of the strike. This brought to an end the first national coal strike and the largest single stoppage that had ever occurred in Britain.

Soon after the miners had returned to work, the country was again in the grip of strike fever. A dispute began over the employment of non-union workers in the Port of London, which rapidly led to the National Transport Workers' Federation of London calling a strike of the entire port. The Government thereupon set up a special enquiry, but its proposal was rejected by the employers who were bent on destroying the National Transport Workers' Federation if they possibly could. The Federation now tried to bring out every port worker in the country, but the response was poor and the Federation had to order its members back to work.

The failure of the Transport Workers' Federation had exposed the weakness of strike action and by the time the 1912 Trades Union Congress was held there was a different atmosphere. Two resolutions raised the issue of syndicalism at the Congress and the voting on them was an overwhelming defeat for Tom Mann and his followers. Syndicalism had been rebuffed, but the question of industrial unionism was far from dead.

The supporters of amalgamation and industrial unionism could point to a solid achievement when, after a long series of negotiations, a National Union of Railwaymen was created out of three separate unions organising manual workers on the railways. The Webbs were so impressed by the establishment of this new industrial union that when they revised their *History of Trade Unionism* they confidently forecast that this would become the new model. In fact, over fifty years later it remains a lone example of the deliberately created industrial union. Moreover, the N.U.R. has still to convince members of the other two unions that it would be in their interests to abandon their organisations in favour of joining an industrial union for the railways.

In 1912 the militant section of the trade-union movement launched a newspaper which they named the *Daily Herald*. This development in Labour journalism grew out of a scheme which had been proposed by the London Society of Compositors and first discussed at the T.U.C. in 1907. During a strike of the London printing trade unions in 1911, to secure a 48-hour week, the London Society of Compositors published a four-page strike sheet which appeared daily during the four months of the stoppage. When the strike ended the publishers of the paper decided to keep it going by a scheme, similar to that employed by George Potter, when he founded *The Beehive*, to raise capital by the issue of five-shilling shares.

The establishment of the *Daily Herald* caused some consternation in the leadership of the Labour Party, since the two men behind the paper, H. W. Hobart and T. E. Naylor, were close to the syndicalists in their outlook and their venture was strongly supported by other militant members of the trade-union movement. The Labour Party Executive Committee decided it should have a newspaper of its own and it asked the Parliamentary Committee if it could have the same facility as had been granted to the proprietors of the *Daily Herald* to address the Congress. In the following year the Parliamentary Committee, much to the anger of the leaders of the Labour Party, accepted an invitation to be represented on the board of directors of the *Daily Herald*. This decision, which was made largely because the new secretary of the T.U.C., C. W. Bowerman, had been a senior official of the London Society of Compositors, proved extremely embarrassing to the Parliamentary Committee, which decided to withdraw its support from the *Daily Herald* when the Labour Party started its own paper, the *Daily Citizen*, in 1913. The *Herald* had by this time become mainly a propaganda journal, publishing articles by syndicalists, guild socialists, distributists and other militant socialist sectarians. The *Daily Citizen* was more orthodox in its format, providing a wide coverage of general news like the other dailies, but supporting the policies of the Labour Party and the unions in their day-to-day struggles. It soon became a casualty of the war, leaving the *Daily Herald* to survive and eventually to become the official voice of the trade unions and the Labour Party.

The financial support which the trade unions had been able to give the Labour Party had been a vital factor in the build-up of the Party's strength in the House of Commons. Members of Parliament had to depend either on a private income or on stipends paid by organisations. Until 1909 the trade unions had not considered that there was any legal impediment to their using their general funds for the purpose of subsidising Labour Members of Parliament. However, in 1908 the secretary of the Walthamstow Branch of the Amalgamated Society of Railway Servants, W. W. Osborne, had brought an action to test his contention that the executive committee of the union had no power to levy members one shilling a year to cover the cost of parliamentary representation. The union had taken eminent counsel's opinion as to the legal validity of the rule and had been advised that the rule did not conflict with the law. The Judge who heard Osborne's action took the same view as the counsel and found in favour of the Society. However, this decision was reversed in the Court of Appeal. The union then appealed to the House of Lords which upheld the finding of the Court of Appeal. It did so on the grounds that trade unions were bodies created by legislation and they could therefore only act in accordance with the provisions laid down in the statute. The Lords found that the 1876 Act did not mention political activities or the use of union funds to subsidise political candidates. It was, therefore, unlawful for the unions to use their funds in this way.

This decision by the House of Lords came as a considerable surprise to the unions since they had been financing political activities for a very long time and some thirty-four years had elapsed since the passing of the 1876 Act before their right to do so had been challenged. The possible implications of the Osborne judgment were far-reaching, for if strictly applied it would rule out many activities the unions had taken for granted they could engage in. By inference it was even doubtful whether affiliation to the T.U.C., whose function was primarily political, was now lawful.

There was a section of the unions that was not displeased with the Osborne decision since they wished to see support for the Labour Party brought to an end. When the issue was discussed at the annual Congress a resolution calling for legislation to reverse the Osborne decision was passed by an enormous majority. The Liberal Government was not in any hurry to rescue the Labour Party from its predicament, but the Government was anxious to retain Labour support after the election of 1910, since its huge majority had been wiped out and it was dependent on the Irish Nationalists and Labour Party members. The Government therefore decided that Members of Parliament should henceforth be paid a salary. This decision was welcomed by the Labour Party and the trade unions since they had advocated this policy for a long time. Nevertheless the 1911 Congress made clear that the unions were not willing to give up their right to engage in political activities in exchange for parliamentary salaries. Continued pressure on the Government eventually persuaded it to introduce a Bill that would remedy the decision of Courts in the Osborne case. The employers also brought a good deal of pressure to bear on the Government and sought to have the unions made liable for damages for procuring a breach of contract.

The Trade Union Act which was eventually passed in 1913 was not entirely to the liking of the unions, since it compelled them to secure the approval of a majority of their members before they could establish a political fund. It also allowed union members to contract out of paying the political contribution without incurring any disability or disadvantage otherwise than concerned with the management of the political fund from which they might be excluded.

The problem which faced the unions and the Labour Party was well put to the Trades Union Congress by J. R. Clynes, a senior official of the National Union of Gasworkers and General Labourers and a member of the Labour Party Executive Committee:

There is the foolish impression that this Bill was offered to us by the Liberal Government. The reverse is the case. This Act represents the most we could extract from them. They would have been glad if we had rejected it. So would the Tories have been glad also.

Although the Labour Party occupied a strategic position it did not wish to vote against the Trade Union Bill, since this might have led to the defeat of the Government and might possibly have brought about its fall. Labour members preferred to try to improve the Bill by amendments and to help the Government defeat Conservative amendments and in this policy they were supported by the Parliamentary Committee.

Support for the syndicalists and militancy had flagged considerably towards the end of 1912 and first part of 1913, but as the Trades Union Congress met in that year the attention of delegates was drawn to a strike that had led to violent clashes with the police in Dublin. Sympathy for the Dublin strikers led the T.U.C. to send a delegation and to launch an appeal for funds to help the strikers' families. The success of this appeal encouraged support for the idea of organising sympathetic action on a national scale if an English union required similar help. The G.F.T.U. had been established for this purpose, but the miners, railwaymen and transport workers were not prepared to participate in action in which the Federation was associated, since they saw it as a major obstacle to the achievement of industrial unionism. These three unions had talked of a joint organisation during the past few years; now, at the suggestion of the miners, they decided to create a triple alliance. Each union pledged that it would support the others and if one went on strike the other two would strike in sympathy.

The establishment of the Triple Alliance changed the balance of power in the trade union movement and threatened to shift initiative from the Parliamentary Committee to a new centre of power and leadership. This development aroused great enthusiasm among those who wished to see the unions involved in a head-on clash with the employers and the state. Unemployment was rising and with it discontent and dissatisfaction. There were many signs that the winter of 1914 might well see an outbreak of serious industrial unrest leading to a general strike. This course of events was prevented by the outbreak of the First World War in August 1914.

4 A Break with the Past, 1914-21

1. THE IMPACT OF WAR

THE period 1914–21 was one of the most eventful in the history of British trade unionism. It was a time of trade union growth and structural change, of mounting industrial conflict, and of ideological ferment. The stimulating force behind these developments was of course war, and the aftermath of war. Before 1914 labour had rarely been in short supply in Britain, so that the bargaining power of trade unions was in normal times strictly limited. This of course was particularly true of those unions catering for unskilled or semi-skilled workers. The war turned this situation on its head. Unlike previous conflicts in which Britain had been engaged, the war which began in 1914 was of so total a character as to require almost complete mobilisation of the nation's manpower resources. As the demand for men to fill the ranks of the armed services mounted inexorably, so the resources of labour at home became scarcer. The domestic economy, with its depleted supply of manpower, had not only to continue to provide the population with basic necessities, but had also to meet the demands of the burgeoning armies for more and more munitions. The pressure on manpower was thus acute, not only was the regular labour force that remained absorbed into full employment, but thousands of women entered the labour market to do the jobs for which men could no longer be spared. With the signing of the Armistice in November 1918 many thought the situation would change. Demobilisation would release many thousands of men for employment at home, and it was felt that the numbers would be too great for the economy to absorb. However, full employment did continue into peace time, at least for a while. The pent up demand, that resulted from the four years of wartime restrictions, issued forth in a great post-war boom that lasted until 1920. The collapse of the boom in that year ended at last the longest spell of full employment British industrial workers had ever known.

The sellers' market for labour generated by the war had profound consequences for the trade-union movement, and therefore for Congress. Initially, however, the official leadership of the movement refused to take advantage of the fact that labour now held the whip hand in the market place. They supported Britain's involvement in the war, and therefore refused to exploit their improved bargaining position through industrial action that would have disrupted production and impaired the war effort. On 24 August 1914 the Parliamentary Committee, acting together with the Labour Party through the Joint Board, proclaimed an industrial truce, and the various union leaderships responded to this call. In March 1915 the official leadership carried their support for the war effort a good deal further by signing the so-called Treasury Agreement with the Government. The Parliamentary Committee and thirty-six unions participated in the talks at the Treasury, which resulted in this agreement. Under its terms the unions formally relinquished the right to strike for the duration of the war, and agreed that all disputes that could not be settled in the normal way should be referred to arbitration. Furthermore, in view of the acute difficulty the Government faced in increasing the output of munitions, the unions undertook to recommend to their members that trade customs be relaxed. This latter point was highly controversial, for it meant the acceptance of 'dilution', that is, the sub-division of skilled jobs so as to permit their performance by semi-skilled workers. Taken as a whole, the concessions made by the unions in the Treasury Agreement were far-reaching, and there was some anxiety when the Government promptly proceeded to give them the binding force of law by passing the Munitions of War Act in July 1915. The commitment of the Labour Movement to the prosecution of the war was further reinforced by the formation of a Coalition Government, in the summer of 1915. It was not without misgivings that the Labour Party agreed to participate in the Government, for with only one member in the Cabinet (Arthur Henderson) and two in junior positions, labour influence upon the two major parties was likely to be strictly limited. They were thus committing themselves to the support of a Government over whose policies they had little control. Nevertheless the Parliamentary Committee supported the Labour Party's action, and this decision was endorsed by Congress.[1]

[1] For a detailed study of the T.U.C. during the war and its aftermath, see Roberts, *The Trades Union Congress, 1868–1921*.

The 1915 T.U.C. held at Bristol (the first since 1913, owing to postponement in 1914) endorsed overwhelmingly the policy of support for the war effort. It was not by all accounts a very inspiring gathering.[1] The war was discussed in terms of conventional patriotic sentiments, and delegates showed little awareness of the problems and opportunities it had created for the movement. The complacency at Bristol belied the tensions that were building up in industry. As the prospect of an early end to the war receded further into the distance, the morale of industrial workers began to break down. There were good reasons for this. While the unions had leant over backwards to accommodate the Government, the latter had done little to protect the workers from the distorting effects of war upon the economy. The cost of living had increased greatly but without a commensurate increase in wage rates. There were numerous other sources of tension; overcrowded housing in munition centres, restrictions on the movement of workers in key industries, and of course dilution. The latter process, sanctioned by the union leaders, was in fact bitterly resisted on the shop floor. Lacking the support of their official leaders in this matter, workers turned increasingly to their local shop stewards who were more prepared to take a militant stand. This was particularly the case in the engineering industry. The pent-up tension finally burst forth in April and May 1917 in a wave of unauthorised strikes that involved nearly all the munitions and shipyard centres of the country. The signal for the stoppage had been a Government proposal to extend the dilution process to private work outside the controlled munitions industry, a proposal that it quickly withdrew in face of the strike wave.[2]

The strike wave of 1917 was something of a turning point. It was a noteworthy fact that the revolt had been entirely led by shop stewards, and owed nothing to the official leadership of the unions. (Shop stewards had played the leading part in an earlier outburst of unofficial strikes in 1915.) In committing themselves so unreservedly to the support of the war effort the union leaders had forfeited the allegiance of large sections of the rank and file, who had at last taken matters into their own hands. This is not to say that the official leaders had not often criticised Government

[1] See the description in Beatrice Webb, *Diaries 1912-24* (1952) pp. 43-4.
[2] For a full study of labour during the war and its aftermath, see W. A. Orton, *Labour in Transition* (1921).

conduct of the war, but that by surrendering their bargaining weapons they had rendered themselves impotent to force a change in policy. However, the decline of morale in industry now stood plainly for all to see, and the Government acted swiftly to retrieve the situation. No doubt events in Russia in the spring of 1917 gave to the Government an added reason for acting quickly to prevent a further deterioration.[1] Food prices were now brought under control, and labour representatives were given important positions in the administration of the new policy. J. R. Clynes became the overall Food Controller. So far as wages were concerned, policy also changed. The arbitration machinery was altered, and whereas wage rates had been held down hitherto, they were now raised over wide areas of the economy. Industrial unrest continued to gather momentum, however, as war weariness took its toll. The Government was under unrelenting pressure on the industrial front, and was obliged to extend the apparatus of economic control over ever widening areas of the economy in order to propitiate a labour force that was in a dangerously rebellious mood.

The great beneficiaries of this situation were the trade unions. Trade-union membership had already been on the increase in the early stages of the war, for full employment had guaranteed would-be unionists against victimisation. Now that industrial action was producing results, new members flocked into the unions. From a total of 4,145,000 in 1914 trade-union membership rose to 6,533,000 in 1918. As full employment continued after the war, and as price inflation continued to menace real wages, so union growth continued, rising to a peak of 8,334,000 in 1920. This level was not to be reached again until after 1945. The 1914–18 war and its aftermath had doubled the numerical strength of the unions. The war affected trade union power in another way. It made for closer working between unions in the same industry, thus paving the way for federation, or even amalgamation. This development resulted from Government regulation of wage rates through its wartime arbitration machinery; the latter lifted wage decisions from local to national level and forced unions in the same industry to act in concert in the presentation of claims. The war thus made for centralisation and co-ordination in the movement, as well as the tremendous increase in overall trade-union membership.

[1] The first phase of the Russian revolution.

2. INTERNATIONAL PERSPECTIVES

The great growth in union power during and immediately after the war took place independently of Congress, which had never been much more than a forum for discussion of general issues, essentially outside the main stream of union activity. The major preoccupations of Congress during the war years were basically the same as those of the Labour Party, indeed the two institutions continually functioned in harness, through their common representation on the Joint Board and various other bodies. In a sense, this co-operation was of considerable significance, for the war had initially strained the trade unions' allegiance to the Labour Party. The character of the latter body, as an alliance of trade unions and socialist societies, had always been productive of tension. The initial impact of war intensified this, for whereas the unions supported the war, the principal socialist society – the I.L.P. – opposed it. At the 1916 Birmingham Congress, the right-wing unionists made a move to bring the Labour Party under the control of the Parliamentary Committee, thus eliminating the influence of the I.L.P. The move was defeated. In the event, the war served to bring the T.U.C. and Labour Party into closer collaboration than ever before. The chief basis for such collaboration was a common concern with war aims. Up until 1915 the unions had given little thought to the purpose of the conflict, but as hostilities dragged on and on, seemingly without end, their uncritical mood evaporated. Such a shift in attitude brought them into closer sympathy with those who had opposed the war from the outset. The central figure in promoting joint T.U.C. and Labour Party effort in working out a war aims policy was Arthur Henderson, Labour Party Secretary. Himself a unionist, Henderson was a powerful force cementing the Labour Alliance, for he stood as a moderating influence between the I.L.P. on the one hand and the trade unions on the other. During the course of 1917 and 1918 the Parliamentary Committee devoted a great deal of its time to broad questions of international policy. This involved it in co-operation not only with the Labour Party, but with Labour and Socialist groups in allied countries. The tangible result of this activity was the 'Memorandum on War Aims', drafted by the British Labour Movement, and adopted by an Allied Labour and

Socialist Conference in February 1918, at which Parliamentary Committee Chairman, J. W. Ogden, presided. The drafting of this memorandum gave British Labour a foreign policy that was distinctive. It was a foreign policy, furthermore, which appealed to liberal minded men of all classes. Henderson had looked beyond a mere military victory, and had thought in terms of a democratic peace settlement, to be safeguarded by a League of Nations. This policy stood in marked contrast to that of the British Government, which was loath to publish any aims beyond the achievement of a complete military victory. The role of the Parliamentary Committee in drawing up the Memorandum had been a secondary one, for the initiative had been largely Henderson's, but it was none the less important. It indicated the shift that was taking place in trade-union policy, towards more active collaboration with the political wing of the movement, including the latter's socialist elements.

The 1918 Congress at Derby (the T.U.C.'s Jubilee Year) endorsed the direction that the Parliamentary Committee's work had taken. Collaboration with the Labour Party on the issue of war aims had in fact taken it further into the realm of international affairs than it had ever ventured before. Such a new departure had not gone unchallenged. Before the war it had been left to the G.F.T.U. to represent the British trade-union movement in international matters, and the Federation resented the intrusion of the T.U.C. into this sphere. Its resentment was all the more because it opposed a war aims policy, clinging instead to an extreme nationalist viewpoint. The Federation in fact provided a platform for rightist elements in the movement, and was unwilling to lose its role in representing the movement internationally. At the 1918 Congress the quarrel between the two bodies was to some extent patched up. It was agreed that in future both organisations should be represented jointly on any delegation sent to an international labour conference. The Parliamentary Committee had, however, firmly established its interest in international affairs, and indeed Congress agreed to its setting up an International Department. It was clearly only a matter of time before the T.U.C. took the field over completely, for it was far more representative of the national movement than was the G.F.T.U., which had only operated in the international sphere by default. In the event, the 1920 Congress was to vote to exclude the G.F.T.U. from participation in international matters, and from then on the T.U.C. had no rival as spokesman for the British movement. The acquisition by the T.U.C. of an international perspective was one of the most important developments of the war years. It led on to T.U.C. involvement in the creation of the International Labour Organisation in 1919, and subsequent participation in that body's activities. It also led to the T.U.C.'s involvement in the work of the International Federation of Trade Unions, a federation of trade union centres, founded just before the war, and reformed in 1919.

The international interests of the Parliamentary Committee had in the war years been closely associated with those of the Labour Party, as we have seen. The Right wing which had opposed T.U.C. intervention internationally, opposed also the link with the Labour Party. In 1916 an attempt had been made to break this link, and at the 1918 Congress this attempt was renewed. The spur which led Lib-Labs like Wilson, Davis and Williams to this final effort was largely provided by internal changes in the nature of the Party. In February 1918 a Labour Party Conference had adopted a new constitution which for the first time formally committed the Party to socialism. The new constitution also provided for the setting up of constituency organisations, a move which promised to increase the middle-class, non-trade union elements in the Party. These developments led Davis to move a resolution at Congress instructing the Parliamentary Committee to form a trade-union 'Labour Party'. The resolution was over-whelmingly defeated. Although distrust of middle-class socialists was still common enough among trade unionists, few were prepared to carry it to the point of open breach. While the relationship of the trade unions to the Labour Party was not always to be harmonious in the years that lay ahead, it was not again to be fundamentally challenged. However, the new Labour Party constitution did have important implications for the unions. In the early days of the Party the trade unions had co-operated with the socialist societies while, in the main, not sharing their belief in socialism. When the Party adopted a socialist constitution in 1918 all affiliated trade unions became theoretically committed to socialism. To some unionists this was an unwelcome development, but they were a declining force in the councils of Congress. The fundamental assumptions of the British trade union movement were increasingly to be of a socialist character. As a recent writer on the labour movement has argued, the prestige of democratic socialism was at its highest in the years that immediately followed World War I.[1] Belief was strong that socialism provided the key to the future development of society. This belief had been immeasurably strengthened by wartime developments, in which the state had been forced to intervene on an unprecedented scale in the workings of the capitalist economy. Furthermore, wartime sacrifices, and the example of the Russian and other revolutions, had generated among many workers an appetite for radical change, a determination not to return to the pre-1914 order. In the main it was to the Labour Party that working people looked as the instrument capable of transforming capitalist society; the working-class movement while increasingly socialist in its assumptions, remained constitutional in character.

3. A TRADE-UNION CENTRE

The tendency after the war to regard the future of society in terms of a confrontation between Capitalism and Socialism was reinforced by party political developments. During the war a split had occurred in the Liberal Party so that after the 1918 election the Labour Party emerged as the chief opposition to the Conservatives. It was against this background that MacDonald was later to declare: 'There are only two parties in politics today. There is the Capitalist Party and the Labour and Socialist Party'.[2] The rising prestige of the Labour Party inevitably affected the role of the T.U.C. Historically the preoccupations of Congress had been largely political in character. During the war, as we have seen, this preoccupation continued, entailing close working with the Labour Party. But with a fully developed political arm there was increasingly less need for the T.U.C. to function as a political pressure group. It was evident that some rationalisation of function had become necessary between the T.U.C. on one hand and the Labour Party on the other. Basically this meant that the T.U.C. should develop the purely industrial side of its work, and concentrate on co-ordinating the policies of its affiliated unions in their dealings with employers, leaving to the Labour Party the functions of

---

[1] Robert Skidelsky, *Politicians and the Slump* (1967) p. 37.
[2] Ibid. p. 37.

promoting the interests of Labour at Westminster. While this seemed to be a rational division of function between the two arms of the Labour Movement, in fact the T.U.C. was in 1918 hardly equipped to fulfil the role of a real central co-ordinating body for the industrial wing.

The term 'T.U.C.' still referred essentially to the annual gathering of delegates, rather than to a central trade union organisation which functioned continuously. The Parliamentary Committee, which maintained continuity between the annual meetings, was composed of union officials who only devoted part of their time to T.U.C. business. Even the Parliamentary Committee Secretary combined his job with that of an M.P.; indeed, given the essentially political character of Congress, this was viewed as a desirable practice. Until the First World War the Secretary had only had one clerk to assist him in carrying out the work of Congress; between them they constituted the complete T.U.C. establishment! The war had, of course, brought changes. Harry Gosling during his Presidential Address to the 1916 Congress had drawn attention to the fact that while the work of the T.U.C. had considerably expanded, there had been no increase in staff to handle this work. Gosling was clearly looking forward to the creation of a real trade-union centre, adequately housed, staffed and financed. 'We must not be satisfied,' he stated, 'until organised Labour is as important in its greater and more national aspects as any Department of State, with its own block of offices and civil service, commodious and well appointed.' Those, like Ernest Bevin, who had seen the splendid headquarters which the T.U.C.'s American counterpart, the American Federation of Labour, was building in Washington, shared Gosling's concern at the lack of a real trade-union centre in Britain.[1] As a result of Gosling's initiative some tentative steps were taken. The T.U.C. moved into new and more commodious office premises in Eccleston Square, but more important was the appointment in 1918 of a full-time Assistant Secretary, who was not an M.P. The post went, significantly, to a socialist, Fred Bramley, organiser for

---

[1] In later years Bevin, no doubt influenced by his American experience decided to build a combined headquarters for his own union, the T.U.C. and the Labour Party. This building, known of course as Transport House, was opened in 1928. See A. Bullock, *The Life and Times of Ernest Bevin 1881–1940* (1960) vol. 1, pp. 405–7.

the National Amalgamated Furnishing Trades Association. For the first time the T.U.C. had acquired a full-time officer, whose energies could be solely devoted to building up a central organisation. Another wartime development, as we have seen, was the international work undertaken by the T.U.C. So far as the industrial side of this work was concerned, the Parliamentary Committee had in July 1918 convened a special conference of unions affiliated to international federations, 'with the object of considering the desirability of making the Parliamentary Committee the British centre for dealing with International Trade Union matters.' As a result it was agreed that a department should be developed by the T.U.C. for collecting and distributing information on international industrial matters. Here is the beginning of the notion that it is a function of a trade-union centre to service its affiliated organisations, by the provision of information and research facilities; it being beyond the resources of each individual union to provide these facilities for itself. After the war the T.U.C. to a considerable extent concentrated its international activities upon the purely industrial side, dis-affiliating from the essentially political Second International, on which the Labour Party was represented, and focusing its interest instead upon the I.F.T.U. In this respect it was thus moving towards a rational division of function between itself and the Labour Party. Even allowing for wartime developments, however, the T.U.C. remained in 1918 inadequately equipped to act as a co-ordinating body for the industrial movement. Such a situation sprang, of course, from the attitude of the affiliated members. Individual unions had always shown the greatest reluctance to delegate power and influence to the centre, and the T.U.C. had only survived as an institution for so long because it had not attempted to encroach upon union autonomy. However, in the period immediately following the Armistice certain influences began to work strongly in favour of a strengthening of the central body, and to these we will now turn.

The idea of a strong central co-ordinating authority for the industrial movement drew strength from what appeared to contemporary unionists to be a dominant tendency in social organisation; namely, the tendency towards greater centralisation. In industry this tendency was manifested in the process of concentration into larger units of production, and the formation of giant multi-plant companies. Alongside this development was the growth of powerful employers' associations, covering whole industries, on a nationwide basis. This process had gone farther in the United States than in Britain, but British trade unionists saw developments in America as an indication of the direction in which capitalist industry was moving in all countries, Britain included. It was this process of concentration in industry which seemed to foreshadow the coming of the socialist state, with the giant private monopolies ultimately being taken into public ownership. During the war the Government had in fact temporarily taken over several industries, such as coal and railways, and had intervened directly in many more. Pending the permanent extension of public ownership, however, it seemed clear to many unionists that the increasing concentration and centralisation of capitalist economic power necessitated a similar movement on the side of organised labour. Only by concentrating its power could the latter act as a countervailing force to large-scale capitalist industry. This need had long been stressed by socialist elements in the trade-union movement, but only limited headway had been made before the war. During the war, however, as we have seen, considerable progress was made in achieving closer working between the various unions: a number of federations were formed, and after the Armistice there were a number of important union mergers resulting in the creation of very large organisations such as the Amalgamated Engineering Union and the Transport and General Workers Union. This progress in consolidating the forces of labour was to some extent offset as a result of the vast increase in union membership which took place in the years up to 1920, for many of the new recruits formed their own unions rather than joining those already in existence, thus multiplying the number of separate organisations and intensifying the problem of co-ordinating union activity. In any case, even allowing for progress made through federation and amalgamation in particular industries, one obvious defect stood out; there was no single directing authority for the movement as a whole. At the head of the movement was a power vacuum, and the efforts at co-ordination lower down served to focus attention on this fact. Thus Ernest Bevin described the trade-union movement in 1919 as 'a great shapeless mass, all the time struggling to co-ordinate its efforts, but finding itself without a head to direct.' Several years after this observation had been made,

T.U.C. officials spelt out the logic of the situation as they saw it:

The tendency towards centralisation which has been so strongly manifested in recent years cannot be without its effect upon the T.U.C. The need is continually felt for some central body able to speak and act authoritatively on behalf of the whole British trade union movement. The T.U.C. is pre-eminently the body which could assume that function.

The need for an authoritative trade-union centre manifested itself in two main ways after 1918. In the first place, the absence of such a centre meant that organised labour failed to make the most of its strong bargaining position during the short post-war boom. Labour's post-war offensive took the form of numerous unco-ordinated strikes during 1919 and 1920, and while many of these were certainly successful in securing higher wages and shorter hours, they did not secure a permanent improvement in the status of the worker in industry. In other words, the gains made were of a short-term character and likely to be quickly undermined once the boom broke. On the other hand, the opportunity to fundamentally alter conditions of employment was missed. To a considerable degree this was because the industrial labour movement had no agreed strategy. In December 1918 Lloyd George's Coalition Government was returned to power with a large majority. It was basically Conservative in composition, and its strategy on the labour front was to play for time. That is, not to reject Labour's more fundamental demands outright, thus provoking an industrial crisis, but to give the appearance of reasonableness until the tide of industrial unrest had died down, and then act to restore the pre-1914 order. In February 1919 it called a National Industrial Conference, with the apparent objective of promoting a better climate of industrial relations. The Conference was representative of the unions and employers. The attitude of the union movement towards the Conference was divided, as it had been earlier to the proposals of the Government's Whitley Committee in 1917. The latter had sought to improve the status of the worker by giving unions more say in general matters affecting industry, aside from wages and hours. It had proposed the setting up of Joint Councils for each industry, with subsidiary bodies at the level of the district and the individual firm. The Report had been accepted by the Government, but reactions to it among unionists were mixed and the T.U.C. had failed to take any definite line on the matter. For the left-wing elements Whitleyism appeared to be an attempt to wean the workers away from demands for real workers' control, and to fob them off with insubstantial schemes of joint consultation. So now with the Industrial Conference. A section of the movement agreed to participate, but the three powerful groups who formed the Triple Alliance – the Miners, Railwaymen, and Transport Workers – opted out. They saw the Conference, with some justification, as a piece of deception by the Government aimed at heading off union militancy. The union element that remained in the discussions put forward some extremely constructive proposals advocating Government action to maintain full employment, both through public works policies, and through the establishment of legal wage minima as a means of raising effective demand. In view of the importance of the unemployment issue between the wars, these proposals are obviously of considerable interest, but in 1919 the weight they carried was limited, not least because they did not have the backing of the whole union movement. Of course, the Miners and others who boycotted the talks were probably quite right in their distrust of the Government's sincerity in convening the Conference, and indeed the unions involved in the talks themselves finally withdrew in 1921 disgusted at the Government's prevarication. But to what extent had the Government been able to get away with these tactics precisely because it had not had to deal with a united and determined trade union movement? Furthermore, if the movement as a whole was not prepared to push its programme through the Industrial Conference, neither was it prepared to rally round the Miners in their uncompromising stand.

At the beginning of 1919 the Miners had demanded the nationalisation of the coal industry and its democratic control by the workers of that industry. The Government had played for time by appointing a Royal Commission to investigate the matter, and when later it felt strong enough to openly reject the Miners' demands, the latter were unable to obtain support from other unions in forcing the issue. The Government's rejection of nationalisation had been made public in August 1919. After consultation with their Triple Alliance partners the Miners had agreed not to strike immediately, but to refer the matter first to the Annual T.U.C. in Glasgow in September. At Glasgow the Miners moved a resolution asking Congress 'to co-operate with the Miners' Federation of Great Britain to the fullest extent with a view to compelling the Government to adopt the scheme of national ownership and joint control recommended by the majority of the Commission in their report.'[1] Such a resolution implied that general strike action might be taken to force the Government's hand. A section of the Miners' leaders fervently believed that a general strike would lead to the defeat of the Government and this would be the first step towards the overthrow of the capitalist system. Faced with this proposal, and understanding its implication, Congress compromised. The Parliamentary Committee agreed that if the Government continued in its refusal to accept nationalisation, then it would convene a special Congress which would then decide upon the action to be taken. Such a special Congress did in fact meet in December 1919: all it decided, however, was that an educational campaign should be waged on behalf of nationalisation of the mines. This rather tame outcome, which was accepted by the Miners, reflected the fact that they had been outmanoeuvred by their supposed ally, the National Union of Railwaymen. The latter had staged its own strike just after the Glasgow Congress, against the wage proposals put forward by the Government. It might have been expected that the N.U.R. and M.F.G.B. would have been careful to co-ordinate their actions, in view of the fact that they both operated in industries still under Government control, that they were both theoretically committed to a nationalisation programme, and that they were formally linked through the Triple Alliance. But the Railwaymen's leader, J. H. Thomas, was a moderate. He was not interested in pressing the Railwaymen's nationalisation claims, and in turn he did not want his union to be involved in a massive struggle with the state for the nationalisation of the mines. When the Government's tough line in wage negotiations necessitated industrial action on the railways, Thomas deliberately acted without reference to the Miners. By the time the special Congress assembled in December the railway strike had been successfully terminated. The Miners could hardly ask for sympathetic strike action by the N.U.R. when the latter had just conducted a successful strike on its own account, without the assistance of the M.F.G.B.

[1] The Royal Commission had supported the Miners' demand for nationalisation by a narrow majority.

The propaganda campaign decided upon in December was of course a failure, as the Miners had expected it would be, but when another special Congress was called in March 1920, the unions were no more willing than before to support massive strike action on behalf of the nationalisation of the mines. The Miners' proposal that direct action be used to this end was overwhelmingly defeated. The weight of Congress opinion was that such a change in ownership could only be brought about by political action through the Labour Party. Realising that alone they were not strong enough to enforce nationalisation upon the Government, the Miners were forced by this decision to limit their industrial activities to wage and hour issues. There was of course an issue of principle involved in Congress's refusal to support the Miners. The growth of the Labour Party meant that there was a real prospect of achieving major social and economic changes by parliamentary means. Such a prospect had been partially clouded immediately after the war by the overwhelming electoral triumph of Lloyd George's Government in 1918. Subsequent Labour Party success in local government elections had revived to a considerable extent earlier expectations. With this prospect in view most trade-union leaders were loath to sanction direct action for what were basically political objectives, such as nationalisation. It was argued, especially by trade-union leaders active in the political movement, men like Thomas and Clynes, that direct action was a double-edged weapon. If Labour used it, it was also open to other groups in the community to use it should a Labour Government ever assume office. During the summer of 1920 the Labour movement did indeed come near to employing industrial action for a political objective, when it seemed for a moment that the Government was leading the country into war with Russia. The crisis passed, however, without any action being taken. It was the nearest the movement ever came to politically motivated industrial action.

The failure of the Miners' campaign for nationalisation reflected the overall failure of the trade-union movement to secure fundamental changes in the conduct of industry during the aftermath of war. It had not secured moderate objectives, such as the thoroughgoing application of the Whitley Committee scheme to industry, or the full-employment policies discussed at the Industrial Conference, or the establishment of a National Industrial Council, also discussed by the Conference. Nor of course had it achieved the objectives of public ownership and workers' control cherished particularly by the more left-wing elements. It had had no programme of realisable objectives and no agreed strategy for attaining them. Even the crucial question of whether industrial action might be legitimately employed for objectives of a political character had been hotly disputed, although as we have seen, Congress ruled it out of court in the Miners' case in 1920. In that year the boom broke, and the trade unions found themselves on the defensive in a world that was uncomfortably like that of pre-1914. Perhaps failure to make any far-reaching change was inevitable given the composition of the Coalition Government, and its determination to avoid any radical change in the existing economic order. But it was obvious that Labour had not played its cards well, that it had lacked 'a head to direct'. Here then was the first of the two ways in which the need for an authoritative trade union centre stood revealed in the aftermath of war.

The second way was more clear-cut. One consequence of the tendency towards centralisation and concentration on both sides of industry was that stoppages became wider in scope. Employers' associations covering whole industries confronted single unions or federations of unions, likewise covering whole industries. Bargaining tended to be nation wide in scope for each industry. A breakdown in negotiations could thus mean a national strike or lock-out tying up an entire industry. This tendency had been clearly apparent before 1914, with a national engineering lock-out in 1897, a national coal strike in 1912, and so on. After the war likelihood of large-scale strikes appeared even greater in view of the growth and consolidation of union membership since 1914. Yet the large-scale stoppage was an obviously clumsy weapon, especially from the labour point of view. It had wide ramifications outside the particular industry in which it was called. This was particularly the case in key industries such as coal or railways, where a stoppage threw thousands out of work in occupations not connected with the dispute. The widespread consequences of a national stoppage seemed to call in question the wisdom of each union continuing to employ the strike weapon purely at its own discretion, without regard to the consequences to other unions. If the large-scale strike was to continue to be employed, there seemed to be good grounds for unions in the various industries acting in concert, as each would in any case be affected by the action of the others. This idea had been in the minds of the founders of the Triple Alliance of railway, mine and road and port transport workers. The national rail strike in the autumn of 1919 had, however, as we have seen, shown the Triple Alliance to be completely ineffective in co-ordinating industrial action as between these three crucial industries. But the rail strike did more than expose the weakness of the Triple Alliance. It led directly to an attempt to invest in the T.U.C. the power to co-ordinate industrial action, not merely for the three Triple Alliance industries, but for the movement as a whole. In the last analysis therefore it was the implications of the large scale strike which provided the *immediate* incentive to develop the T.U.C. as an authoritative national trade-union centre.

4. THE CREATION OF THE GENERAL COUNCIL

The 1919 rail strike set in motion a sequence of events that led directly to the reorganisation of the T.U.C. and its emergence in something like the form we know it today. The strike had been brought to an end through the intervention of a Mediation Committee hurriedly set up by the Transport Workers, on the initiative of Ernest Bevin. The necessity for the formation of such a Committee sprang from the absence of any regular body in industry capable of taking the initiative in bringing about a settlement of an important dispute. Bevin and others thought that this function, together with the whole business of co-ordinating industrial action, should be the concern of a reformed Parliamentary Committee, adequately staffed and equipped to act as a centre for the industrial movement. His Mediation Committee therefore approached the Parliamentary Committee when the strike was over, with a view to getting something done to end the anarchy in trade union affairs. The Parliamentary Committee appointed a sub-committee to consider the matter, and this met with Bevin's group, and also the trade union side of the National Industrial Conference. These three bodies then merged to form a Trade Union Co-ordination Committee. The Committee included the most creative elements in the Labour movement, drawn mainly from the trade unions naturally, but including also Arthur Henderson, Labour Party Secretary, and G. D. H. Cole of the Labour Research Department, both of whom came in through their representation on the Labour side of the Industrial Conference. Among trade unionists

c

the Committee included Gosling, who had as T.U.C. President in 1916 strongly advocated the development of the T.U.C.'s role, Bevin, and Bramley, the full time T.U.C. Assistant Secretary. Bramley acted as the Committee's Secretary. The Committee quickly brought under review all the issues connected with the development of a trade-union centre, and by December 1919 it had the outlines of a scheme ready, which it submitted to the Special Congress summoned in that month to consider the problems of the miners. The delegates accepted the report of the Co-ordination Committee and gave it a mandate to work out further details. When Congress assembled for its regular annual meeting in Portsmouth in September 1920 the detailed scheme was more or less complete.

The Co-ordination Committee scheme provided in the first instance for the creation of a General Council to replace the Parliamentary Committee. The General Council was to be larger in size than its predecessor, and was to be endowed with greater responsibilities, particularly in the industrial as against the political sphere. It was to consist of thirty members, elected under a grouping system that had been devised by G. D. H. Cole. Under Cole's scheme the unions affiliated to Congress were to be divided into 17 industrial groups, each of which was to be allocated a certain number of seats on the Council. Each group was to nominate the candidates for its quota of seats, but the vote was to be taken by Congress as a whole. This scheme of election was designed to strengthen the authority of the central body, by making it more fully representative of the various industrial interests attached to Congress. So far as the responsibilities of the new body were concerned, the Co-ordination Committee proposed that they be defined in the following terms:

(a) The General Council shall keep watch on all industrial movements, and shall attempt, where possible, to co-ordinate industrial action.

(b) It shall promote common action by the trade union movement on general questions, such as wages and hours of labour, and any other matter of general concern that may arise between trade unions and employers or between the trade union movement and the government, and shall have power to assist any union which is attacked on any vital question of trade union principle.

(c) Where disputes arise, or threaten to arise, between trade unions it shall use its influence to promote a settlement.

(d) It shall assist trade unions in the work of organisation, and shall carry on propaganda with a view to strengthening the industrial side of the movement and for the attainment of any or all of the above objects.

(e) It shall enter into relations with the trade-union and labour movements in other countries with a view to promoting common action and international solidarity.

In order that the new Council would be adequately staffed and equipped to carry out these duties, the Committee proposed an increase in the affiliation fees to meet the cost of improved facilities.

Here then were the essentials of the Co-ordination Committee scheme. In itself, it must be admitted that it altered the nature of Congress very little. This was because the proposed General Council, like the Parliamentary Committee already in existence, lacked any executive authority over affiliated unions. There was to be no transference of power to the centre, no limitation of individual union autonomy, as was made clear by Harry Gosling in moving the acceptance of the scheme. For what then did all the new responsibilities of the central body count, if it had no directive power over the movement? Some delegates were not slow to raise this question. The new General Council, they argued, would have no power to co-ordinate anything; it would merely be the old Parliamentary Committee writ large. There was, however, an element of insincerity about this criticism, which Ernest Bevin, as one of the authors of the scheme, was quick to fasten on. It was all very well for the delegates to attack the vagueness of the Council's powers, but would they have liked the scheme any better if the General Council *had* been given powers that infringed union autonomy? It was because the Co-ordination Committee was only too well aware of the opposition that any such infringement would have aroused that it had decided to tread warily. Bevin explained the Committee's approach to the problem in these terms:

It is true that the Co-ordination Committee has not attempted to lay down an actual final, detailed plan as to how this new thing will work out. It would be a mistake if we did. There is no finality in our conception of organisation. But we realise that there is greater danger in trying, before we are allowed to create confidence by the existence of a body, to ride rough shod over the natural conservatism of our movement.

It was in this spirit that Bevin and Gosling were to carry through their own Transport Workers' amalgamation the following year. They did not expect to revolutionise the movement overnight. The creation of a General Council would be a beginning. The Council would have to proceed by creating confidence in the leadership it gave to the movement. It would have to feel its way at first, exercising its authority in fields where this proved to be practicable, and abandoning lines of development that proved to be unrewarding. The exact nature of its ultimate authority could not be predicted and laid down in advance.

The 1920 Congress accepted the Co-ordination Committee scheme, although it was not until a year later that the first General Council was elected. In the interval the Co-ordination Committee turned its attention to relationships with the Labour Party. The problem of reorganising the T.U.C. had from the beginning been closely related to the development of the Labour Party, for, as we have seen, the latter's rise had made the political functions of the Parliamentary Committee largely obsolete. The issue of the new General Council's relationship with the political wing arose at two levels. First of all, there was the problem of equipping the central body with an adequate full time staff. One aspect of this question was the need for a T.U.C. research department, for hitherto the Parliamentary Committee had had to rely on an outside, voluntary body, the Labour Research Department. The Co-ordination Committee decided that in the development of office facilities for the General Council it would be desirable to provide some services on a joint basis with the Labour Party. As both bodies required research and other facilities it appeared wasteful for each to develop their own departments. After the 1920 Congress details were therefore worked out for the establishment of a joint Labour Party/T.U.C. arrangement. The Labour Party already had under its control staff employed on research, publicity, and international matters, and it was proposed that this should form the basis for three new joint departments. In addition a joint legal department was to be formed. In the event, the legal section was not developed, but International Research and Publicity Departments began operation on a joint basis in January 1922. At this time the Labour

Party and T.U.C. shared adjoining premises in Eccleston Square.

The initiative for these joint staffing arrangements had come largely from the Labour Party side, and from Arthur Henderson, the Party's Secretary in particular. At one stage Fred Bramley felt the politicians were using steam-rollering tactics, and commented on one of their memoranda – 'They just make plans and ask us for endorsement.' Henderson was in fact very keen for a close link between the T.U.C. and the Labour Party and his interest went beyond staffing arrangements to include questions of policy determination. This latter was the second of the two levels of relationship mentioned above. In November 1920 Henderson proposed the formation of a National Joint Council, composed of representatives of the General Council, the Labour Party Executive, and the Parliamentary Labour Party. In Henderson's eyes the National Joint Council was to be rather more than a replacement for the old Joint Board. For him the T.U.C. and the Labour Party were merely branches of one organic Labour Movement. This Labour Movement needed a supreme head, which could co-ordinate the activities of the industrial and political wings and prevent overlapping and conflicting functions and policies, just as within the industrial section the General Council was supposed to co-ordinate the activities of individual unions. Henderson wrote:

There is an urgent need for some joint body which shall have regard to the interests of the Labour movement as a whole. From the point of view of the political side of the movement, it is vital that it should be brought into consultation in the case of great industrial disputes, not for the purposes of intervention, but in order that the political considerations involved should be fully realised. Moreover, the Party cannot regard without considerable concern the tendency of the T.U.C. to embark upon the formation of policy on political questions. It is desirable that the Labour Party Conference and the T.U.C. should as far as possible each keep within their own sphere and that where questions arise affecting both, they should speak with a single voice.

The single voice was to be provided by the National Joint Council. In Henderson's original scheme it was also to control directly the joint T.U.C./Labour Party departments, thus giving it and them a status independent of both the Labour Party Executive and the General Council. This aspect of the scheme was, however, vetoed by the T.U.C. The main proposal for the creation of a National Joint Council was accepted at the 1921 Cardiff Congress, and the Council held its first meeting on 18 November 1921. Like the General Council itself, its authority was ill-defined; it could be everything or nothing. Its creation, however, to some extent reflected the concern in the ranks of Labour politicians lest the establishment of a General Council should result in an increased reliance by the unions on large-scale industrial action. They feared that direct action might cut across the Labour Party's efforts to achieve power constitutionally. At the 1920 Congress, for example, J. R. Clynes, a trade unionist prominent in the Labour Party, had moved the reference back of the Co-ordination Committee's report and proposed instead that a new scheme be devised to incorporate the industrial and political wings into one organisation. Clynes was defeated of course, but his proposal had some resemblance to that put forward by Arthur Henderson for the formation of a National Joint Council. In both there was the desire that the political wing should exercise some influence over the industrial.

The first General Council was elected at the 1921 Congress in Cardiff. The new era in the life of the T.U.C. did not begin auspiciously. There was in the first place a muddle over the actual process of election, so that a second ballot had to be taken. Apart from this, however, and more serious, Congress took two decisions which appeared to severely inhibit the future development of the General Council. The Co-ordination Committee had during the period since the previous Congress come up with the proposal that the chairman of the new Council should be a full-time officer of the T.U.C., appointed by Congress. This was a move which would obviously have strengthened the authority of the central body. For this very reason, however, the unions opposed it. There was also a question of personalities involved. None of the leading trade-union figures relished the exaltation of one of their number into the position of supreme head of the trade-union movement.[1] The second decision concerned the crucial question of the General Council's powers. Arthur Pugh of the Iron and Steel Trades Confederation had moved a resolution to obtain for the Council precise powers to consult with any union involved in a large scale dispute with employers, in order 'firstly to obtain an equitable settlement of the dispute without a stoppage of work, and, secondly,

[1] See Roberts, *The Trades Union Congress, 1868–1921*, p. 352.

failing such a settlement that the machinery and resources of the movement generally may be co-ordinated and applied in such a way as to serve a successful issue'. The proposal was rejected by Congress, principally due to the opposition displayed by some unions to the idea implicit in the first part of the resolution; namely, that their freedom to strike would be limited by the necessity to consult with the General Council. On these grounds Robert Smillie, left-wing leader of the Miners, described the resolution as the most reactionary ever to come before Congress: 'This is a motion proposing to draw the teeth of organised labour and take away its arms.' C. T. Cramp of the Railwaymen attacked it on the same grounds. It was also opposed, of course, by con-servative 'no-change' elements in the movement. The General Council thus began its life with powers and indeed personnel, that were not so very different from the Parliamentary Committee it succeeded. But it also began its life at a time of severe economic crisis, and this fact was to strongly colour the early years of its existence.

5 On the Brink, 1921-6

In 1921 85·9 million working days were lost in industrial disputes, a figure surpassed only once in British history, in 1926, and then only in the unique circumstances of a general strike. The bitter climate of industrial relations during 1921 is perhaps not difficult to explain. Since the end of the war the unions, strengthened by amalgamation and federation, and inflated by vast membership increases, had pushed up money wages and cut the length of the working day. Labour's offensive continued long after the brief post-war boom collapsed, and money wages did not reach their peak until early in 1921, when prices and employment levels were already falling at an alarming rate. In these circumstances the labour offensive led directly into a capitalist offensive, as employers sought to force down labour costs and so recover their profit margins. But the unions were strongly entrenched in industry and determined to retain as far as possible their post-war gains. Head-on clashes between capital and labour thus occurred along almost the entire industrial front, the most dramatic being the national lock-out in the coal industry. After 1921 the struggle abated somewhat, but nevertheless 1922 witnessed a national lock-out in the engineering industry, and 1923 strikes and lock-outs over wage reductions in agriculture, building, and port transport. In conditions of heavy unemployment the unions were certainly fighting a losing battle, and money wages were cut sharply, but they did not fall so fast as the cost of living, so that for those who retained their employment real wages in fact rose. Furthermore, the unions were in the main successful in preserving intact the shorter working day they had gained just after the war.

By 1924 the worst of the slump appeared to be over, employment was improving, and prices at last began to turn upwards. In this situation there were some attempts by the unions to recover wages lost since 1920, most notably a national dock strike called by Ernest Bevin's powerful new Transport and General Workers

Union. Employment levels did not, however, improve further after 1924, leaving about a million men still without work. There was thus no renewed labour offensive during the twenties. Instead it seemed likely that a period of relative industrial peace would ensue. In 1925, however, Britain returned to the Gold Standard at the pre-war parity, and in so doing over-valued the pound, thus worsening the competitive position of the already ailing export industries. A remedy was sought in the further reduction of labour costs, so that the unions found their standards once more under pressure. Employers in both the coal and textile industries demanded wage cuts, and the Prime Minister, Stanley Baldwin, was said to have told the Miners' leaders, 'all the workers of this country have got to take reductions in wages to help put industry on its feet'. Given the commitment to the Gold Standard at the pre-war parity, the British price level was too high. If it was to be lowered, wages would have to be cut. The miners were adamant against accepting wage reductions, but they had little hope of winning any struggle single-handed. They could, however, claim that in standing out against any worsening of conditions in the coal industry they were fighting not merely their own battle, but that of British wage earners generally. For if cuts were successfully forced on the miners, they would quickly be forced on workers in other industries as well. It was on this basis that the Miners' Federation appealed to the General Council of the T.U.C. for assistance in July 1925.

In 1919 Congress had turned down an appeal by the Miners for assistance; in 1925, however, the General Council promised support. In part the change in policy reflected parallel changes in the policy of the Miners' Federation. In 1919 the T.U.C. was asked to organise industrial action to secure nationalisation of the coal industry. In 1925 the Miners still looked to nationalisation as a long term solution to their problems, but the T.U.C. was being asked only to defend their wage and hour standards. It was a straightforward industrial issue, with no political overtones. But there was more than this to the T.U.C.'s change of policy. Ever since the creation of the General Council, in 1921, the issue of whether or not it should organise assistance for affiliated unions had been subject to constant debate. There were resolutions on the question at every Congress between 1921 and 1925, and the issue forms the central theme running through these years. The momentous decision taken by the General Council in July 1925 must be set against this background.

2. THE BRAMLEY ERA

In the previous chapter we saw how the Cardiff Congress had turned down an attempt to give the General Council wider powers in industry. Despite this setback, the issue remained a live one, owing to the severe pressure being exerted on labour's wage and hour standards in 1921–2. There were, in particular, two General Council members who felt that this pressure was severe enough to justify combined action by the unions in their own defence. The two members in question, both of left-wing sympathies, were Alf Purcell and George Hicks, of the Furnishing Trades and Builders respectively. Their cue for action came with the national lock-out in the engineering trade, in the spring of 1922. At the Council meeting on 21 March Hicks proposed that they should immediately convene a conference of union executives, 'to review the position of Labour in relation to the apparent mass attack upon trade unions, immediately expressing itself through the Engineers.' At the Conference the unions were to be asked to support the Council in any action it might take to defend trade-union standards, including if necessary a 'call for a National Down Tools'. Hicks's motion was seconded by Purcell, but the rest of the Council were cautious. The unions were already being circularised as to their opinions on greater Council powers to co-ordinate resistance, and it was decided to await the replies to this circular before taking any action. In the event, the engineering crisis passed without anything being done by the T.U.C. The General Council was even excluded from a mediating role, owing to the smart intervention of the National Joint Council. A situation much to the satisfaction of Arthur Henderson no doubt, but hardly a flying start for the reorganised trade-union centre.

The activity of Hicks and Purcell in the spring of 1922 was not, however, entirely without effect, for the General Council decided to set up a special Joint Defence sub-committee, to explore further the question of the T.U.C.'s role in industrial disputes. The Committee held its first meeting in April 1922, and continued to function right through until 1925, concerning itself with all the problems involved in the co-ordination of industrial action from the centre. Meanwhile the full General Council had decided to make this a major issue at the 1922 Southport Congress. It tabled a resolution amending the Standing Orders governing its own duties. The amendment followed closely that proposed by Arthur Pugh at Cardiff, and presumably was influenced by the presence of the steel workers' leader on the Council. The amendment proposed in the first instance to make it obligatory 'upon affiliated unions to keep the Council informed with regard to matters arising as between the unions and employers and/or between one union and another'. The Council was not to intervene in any dispute so long as there was a prospect of it being amicably settled, but in the event of negotiations breaking down and a major stoppage being threatened, the Council was to be enabled to take the initiative in calling the unions into consultation and in attempting to secure a settlement. Unions refusing the advice of Council were to be reported to Congress. If, after the intervention of the T.U.C., the policy of the employers forced a stoppage, then the General Council was to be empowered to organise on behalf of the unions involved the necessary 'moral and material' support. The most noticeable thing about this procedure was that it involved potentially a considerable limitation of individual union autonomy. If strictly enforced it would in fact end the unilateral right of each union to strike as and when it saw fit. This was undoubtedly the intention of the amendment, and for good reason. Co-ordination of industrial action on a massive scale implied discipline in the use of the strike weapon. The General Council could not possibly undertake to organise assistance, at a moment's notice, for every union that had got itself involved in a stoppage.

Apart from the amendment to the Standing Orders, outlined above, the General Council made several other proposals to Congress, designed to bring it into closer touch with developments in industry. The unions were asked to forward agreements and documents to the Joint Research Department (operated in conjunction with the Labour Party), and to notify the General Council when disputes occurred. It was also suggested that the Council should obtain from the Research Department a quarterly report on the state of industry, which would be distributed to the unions, 'as a centralised intelligence service is essential if there is to be any combined action in defence of trade union standards'. Taken as a whole, the General Council's 'package' presented to the

Southport Congress bore the strong imprint of Fred Bramley's influence. As full time assistant secretary to Congress since 1918, and secretary of the Co-ordination Committee which had planned the T.U.C. reorganisation, his experience of the central body was unrivalled. He was, furthermore, dedicated to the strengthening of T.U.C. influence. Bowerman, the Secretary, was a figurehead. He was in his seventies, and was in any case distracted from his T.U.C. work by Parliamentary duties.

The 1922 Congress rejected the proposed amendment to the Standing Orders, although it tacitly accepted the other suggestions put forward by the Council. If the price for co-ordination was the transfer of power to the centre the big unions were not prepared to pay it. The Miners, the Railwaymen, the Engineers, and the Transport Workers all opposed the amendment. The most constructive opposition came from the T.G.W.U. Bevin, the General Secretary, was not a member of the General Council until 1925, but he had been active on the Co-ordination Committee and had therefore an interest in the development of the Council's role. Bevin felt that the T.U.C. was still inadequately equipped to perform the functions to which it aspired. As we have seen, the principal officer of Congress, the Secretary, was an M.P. and therefore only devoting part of his time to industrial matters. But even apart from that, the T.U.C. was inadequately staffed. The Co-ordination Committee had originally proposed that six full time secretaries and twelve typists should be appointed to service the General Council. The secretaries were to have been attached to six group sub-committees, into which the Council was divided on the basis of industrial interests. The group sub-committees had been set up as planned, but only one officer, Alec Firth, had been appointed, and he acted as secretary to all the groups. The groups apart, most of the T.U.C. establishment was shared with the Labour Party. The General Council was asking Congress for very wide responsibilities. Bevin felt that it was not yet equipped to cope with them.

Adequately equipped or not, by the autumn of 1922 the General Council was giving a lead to the industrial movement such as had never been forthcoming in Parliamentary Committee days. Its activities were developing over a broad front. At the 1922 Congress it had for example proposed to move into the educational sphere, gradually taking over and merging into one system the various institutions catering for adult working-class students. It had also persuaded Congress to raise affiliation fees in order to permit the taking over of the *Daily Herald* by the Labour movement, so that henceforth the trade-union viewpoint would receive adequate national publicity. So far as its direct role in industry was concerned, a clear strategy was beginning to emerge. It was planned primarily by Bramley and the Joint Defence Committee, of which Hicks was a member. The need to persevere with the attempt to amend the Standing Orders was accepted. However, in so far as it would take time to persuade the movement of the necessity for such an amendment, an immediately constructive role had to be found for the Council. Meeting after the Southport Congress the Defence Committee settled on three objectives: the promotion of a more rational trade-union structure, the carrying on of propaganda and educational activities with a view to strengthening the industrial side of the movement, and the cultivation of closer contact with federations of unions. Each of these three objectives had its special significance for the development of T.U.C. authority in industry.

The question of the Council's role in the matter of structure was an important one, for it could be argued that the effectiveness of the movement was hampered as much by chaotic overlapping and competition between unions as by any weakness in central direction. The main problem was the clash between unions organised on a vertical (or industrial) basis and unions that recruited horizontally across industrial boundaries (craft and general unions). There were not many vertical unions – the Miners' Federation and the National Union of Railwaymen were the principal examples – but they were sufficiently important to make contact with a wide range of craft and general unions, with the inevitable outcome in inter-union disputes. Apart from the clash between horizontal and vertical associations there was also the problem that in Britain competition existed even between unions of the same type, because unlike in America the central organisation had never attempted to lay down the principle of exclusive jurisdiction. In the early twenties, with union membership on the decline, after the collapse of the boom, inter-union disputes reached a new level of intensity, and threatened to undermine the whole solidarity and morale of the movement. The climax came at the 1923 T.U.C. in Plymouth, when the warring unions carried their grievances on to the floor of Congress instead of confining them to the sessions of the General Council's Disputes Sub-Committee. The number of inter-union disputes continued to grow between 1923 and 1924, but at Congress in the latter year any repetition of the Plymouth experience was avoided. The General Council was able to insist that inter-union disputes be confined to the sessions of the Disputes Committee, and the latter set forth certain empirical principles on which to adjudicate cases. As the Committee pointed out to the 1924 Congress, however, it could not pronounce in favour of any one principle of organisation, as it was being asked to do by various unions. In so far as disputes arose out of clashes between differing conceptions of organisation – craft, industrial, general – this was a matter for Congress as a whole to resolve.

The General Council had from the beginning recognised a responsibility to investigate the wider issue of union structure, and in July 1922 it had requested the Joint Research Department to prepare a memorandum on the subject. The Southport Congress went further, passing a resolution calling for a comprehensive report, and the Joint Research Department thereupon initiated a full scale enquiry. While interim reports were issued from time to time, the matter was so fully investigated that the final report was not completed until 1927. The General Council did not, however, remain inactive while the investigation was being conducted. There was scope for initiative from the centre in bringing about amalgamations of unions catering for the same class of workers. Although such initiative was in danger of prejudging the conclusions of the enquiry, the Council already had a rough scheme on which to work. This was provided by the system under which affiliated unions were grouped into various industrial categories for the purposes of electing representatives on to the General Council. The Co-ordination Committee which had framed this system had no doubt envisaged that it might serve as a framework for future union mergers. Between the Southport and Plymouth Congresses the General Council therefore convened amalgamation conferences in the metal trade, textiles, printing and various other sectors. The Council continued to pursue this policy throughout the twenties, though with limited success as we shall see.

The second of the objectives set by the Defence Committee for the Council to pursue concerned its involvement in propaganda activities in industry. It was felt that the central body was in a position to view the needs of the movement as a whole, and should therefore put across to the mass of unionists the general, as opposed to the sectional, view. After the Southport Congress the Council's propaganda activity took the form of a 'Back to the Unions' campaign, designed to arrest the decline in total trade-union membership. The 'Back to the Unions' campaign was not itself a success, indeed it merely exacerbated the competition for membership between rival unions, but it did bring the General Council into touch with the local organs of union activity – the trades councils. After the Plymouth Congress the Joint Defence Committee singled out the trades councils as bodies for the special attention of the T.U.C. It was probably felt that the General Council would never be effective in putting across the case for its having wider powers, unless it could make its influence felt directly upon trade-union opinion. As things stood its only contact with the rank-and-file opinion was through the official machinery of individual unions, but if a permanent link could be forged with the trades councils the central body could develop its own independent channel of communication with the grass roots. At a meeting of the Defence Committee on 20 December 1923 Fred Bramley suggested that the trades councils should be utilised as the local T.U.C. correspondence centres, and that they should be linked with the central organisation by means of a Joint Advisory Council.

There were risks in Bramley's policy, for there was in fact considerable concern in some quarters of the movement as to the activities of the trades councils in the early 1920s. The councils had been disaffiliated from Congress since the 1890s, and since that time had become more and more isolated from the industrial movement. To some extent this had been compensated for by the development of their political activities, but there was still much discontent at the exclusion of the councils from the industrial movement, and in 1922 some councils had begun organising conferences on their own account, on major issues such as the reform of trade-union structure. Such activity outside the official movement was not welcome to many union officers, especially as the councils provided a ready-made sounding board for minority groups – Communists especially. The Defence Committee thus determined to tread warily in this matter. It was proposed to give the trades councils official recognition, but not to admit them into affiliation with the T.U.C. 'Maximum of recognition with safety' was the policy approved at the 20 December meeting. The initial problem the Defence Committee had to face in this sphere was how best to establish contact with the councils, which were scattered in great profusion throughout Britain. Since 1922 there had existed a National Federation of Trades Councils, and this might have seemed the appropriate body through which to act, especially as one of its expressed objects was the strengthening of the powers of the General Council. At this point, however, the ideological issue made its appearance, for the President of the National Federation was Harry Pollitt, a prominent Communist, and the organisation was thus suspect to a large section of the General Council. Instead of operating through the Federation, the Council decided to convene its own conference of major trades councils, and this duly met on 7 May 1924. Fred Bramley addressed the Conference on behalf of the General Council, and proposed that in future there should be a mutual exchange of information between the centre and the localities, and that the trades councils should become circulating agencies for all special propaganda publications issued by the T.U.C. The outcome was that a Consultative Committee, representative of the two sides, was appointed to examine the proposals and report to a further conference. The link with the localities had been forged.

The cultivation of closer contact between the General Council and federations of unions was the third area of Defence Committee policy. The objective was not new in 1922, it dated in fact from 1920, and was derived from the Co-ordination Committee scheme for the reorganisation of Congress. The point was that as the area of industrial disputes widened, so control of policy began gradually to shift from individual unions to federal bodies. These bodies were not represented at Congress, yet they were likely to play an increasingly important part in industrial affairs. Anticipating this development, the Co-ordination Committee had proposed that the six industrial group sub-committees of the General Council should be responsible for maintaining the closest possible links with federal bodies operating in their respective spheres. The idea was that in the first instance the federations could be brought to plan their industrial action in consultation with their respective T.U.C. group sub-committee. It was hoped that in the long run the group sub-committees would themselves take over the functions of the federations, so that control of industrial policy would be concentrated directly in the hands of the General Council. Indeed, shortly after the General Council was set up, a proposal was made that Group A Committee, covering mining and transport, should take over the functions of the discredited Triple Alliance. Nothing however came of the idea. By 1924 in fact the group sub-committees had not shown much sign of development, and an investigation was carried out into their activity. Only Group B had performed any useful work, due largely presumably to the personal composition of the Committee, which included Hicks, Purcell and Pugh. In part, the failure to maintain close contact with industry via a group/federation link sprang from weaknesses in the Co-ordination Committee scheme. The coverage of the Group Committees was too wide. Group B for example covered the iron and steel, shipbuilding, engineering, and building industries. The groups had been fashioned in this way because with 32 Council members only a small number of sub-committees was possible.[1]

The group system was, however, only a means. The end was to bring the General Council into closer contact with the various labour organisations responsible for initiating major movements in industry – whether they were federations or informal groups of unions or even single unions. At the Southport Congress, the unions had been asked to forward agreements and documents to the Research Department and to notify the General Council of disputes. The response to these requests was poor, as the General Council Report for 1924 Hull Congress emphasised:

It is regretted that the General Council is not kept adequately informed of negotiations which are being conducted between unions and employers' associations for the revision of conditions of employment. The Council is sometimes entirely dependent upon Press reports, and disputes of first class importance may be developing, a strike or lock-out may take place, without the Council having first hand knowledge of the circumstances.

The Report stressed the need for the Council to be kept informed regarding all departments of industrial activity participated in by affiliated organisations. To this end it had circularised the unions,

---

[1] For an analysis of the grouping system and other aspects of T.U.C. structure in the twenties, see V. L. Allen, 'Reorganisation of the T.U.C., 1918–1927', *British Journal of Sociology*, xi (1960).

asking them to make one official in each union office responsible for forwarding information. For its part the Council announced its willingness to send representatives to special conferences or annual meetings of affiliated unions, and federations, in order to keep in touch with important developments. Despite its ill-informed condition the General Council did, however, develop its contact, with unions and federations between 1922 and 1924, through judicious intervention in industrial disputes in a mediatory capacity, and with the consent of the unions involved. In the year preceding the Hull Congress it had mediated on disputes in the shipbuilding, dock, railway and engineering industries. This activity demonstrated, the 1924 Report suggested, 'not only the practicability of the General Council being invested with increased powers but that the power sought can be safely exercised.'

The General Council had renewed its request for an amendment to the Standing Orders at the Plymouth Congress, only to have it rejected. At Hull the amendment was moved once more. This time the Council may well have felt more confident of success. Apart from the activities recounted above, which it believed would strengthen the case for central co-ordination, the Council had also done much since 1922 to put its own house in order. In this way it hoped no doubt to meet the kind of argument which Ernest Bevin had brought forward at Southport against greater T.U.C. power. Bowerman had retired as Secretary in 1923, and the Council had brought forward at Congress that year a recommendation that in future the office should not be combined with parliamentary duties, but should be full time in a complete sense. The proposal was accepted, and Fred Bramley was elected to the new post. Bramley's elevation had left vacant the office of Assistant Secretary, and this post was filled in January 1924 with the appointment of Walter Citrine, then Assistant Secretary of the Electrical Trades Union.[1] Citrine was a professional administrator in a sense that very few trade union officers were in those days, and within a short space of time he was overhauling the administrative machine at Eccleston Square. With the office in Citrine's competent hands, Bramley had more time to make his powerful presence felt in the movement outside. They were a formidable

[1] In 1925 Vincent Tewson, like Citrine a future T.U.C. General Secretary, joined the staff as Secretary of the newly established Organisation Department.

combination, and they carried the T.U.C. image a good distance away from what it had been in Parliamentary Committee days. The 1924 General Council report, which was their work, reflected, in its range and sense of direction, the change that had taken place.

The Hull Congress did in fact endorse the Council's application for wider powers. It accepted by a large majority an amendment to the Standing Orders, giving the Council powers to intervene in industrial disputes. The amendment, which was moved on behalf of the Council by George Hicks, was almost identical with that proposed two years earlier at Southport and described above.

3. LEFT-WING INTERLUDE

On the face of it, the decision of the 1924 Congress to amend the Standing Orders was rather remarkable. It had rejected virtually the same amendment in 1921, 1922, and 1923. Undoubtedly the General Council had succeeded in creating greater confidence in its leadership, and this partly accounts for the reversal of Congress policy. To some extent, therefore, the strategy of the Defence Committee may be said to have paid off. But there was more to the reversal of policy than this. The greatest opponents of any T.U.C. control over disputes had in the past been the Miners. Yet at Hull they supported the extension of Council powers. Their new Secretary, left-winger Arthur Cook, actually seconded the amendment. What may have influenced the Miners, and indeed other groups, was their notion as to how the increased powers would be used. It will be remembered that those powers contained two fundamental points. (1) The intervention of the Council to try to settle a dispute without a stoppage. (2) In the event of a stoppage, the mobilisation of the resources of the movement in support of the union or unions involved. In the past, left-wingers and others strongly suspected that the influence of the Council would be primarily exerted to secure the first objective, and in this sense would act against a militant policy. There had, however, always been on the Council elements which took the second objective seriously. We have seen how Hicks tried to mobilise the movement in 1922. In 1924 this element was in the ascendant on the Council. Perhaps this was why the Miners and others were prepared to grant powers which they had firmly withheld in the past.

There is no doubt the years 1924 and 1925 saw a distinct shift to the Left, both on the General Council and at Annual Congress. Impatience of the continued high level of unemployment may well have been responsible for this shift so far as the rank and file of the movement were concerned. There was also the experience of the first Labour Government, which held office during 1924. For many this was a disillusioning experience, in view of the failure of the Government to make any direct impact upon the unemployment problem, or to show itself as being distinctly different from the Administrations that had preceded it.[1] Apart from these general factors, the existence of a Labour Government influenced developments at the T.U.C. in several very definite ways. In the first place it removed from the General Council some of the more moderate individuals, who left to take up Government positions. These included J. H. Thomas, the Railwaymen's leader and a very influential figure in the movement. In the absence of these people, and with the socialist Bramley as the Secretary in place of Bowerman, left-wing elements assumed a much greater prominence on the Council than hitherto. Alf Purcell was President of the 1924 Congress, and another left-winger, Alonzo Swales, an engineer, was President in 1925 at Scarborough. The prominence of the Left on the Council was, as has been suggested above, probably partly responsible for the granting of increased powers in 1924. Secondly, the experience of Labour Government strengthened the hand of those who had long argued that the wage earners must rely primarily upon their direct industrial power, rather than upon Parliamentary pressure, in the short run at any rate. It was this theme that Alf Purcell stressed in his Presidential Address to the 1924 Congress:

As surely as we lift our eyes from the workshop to gaze entirely at Parliament, so surely do we weaken and dissipate our strength in the very place where Capitalism for 8, 9 and 10 hours every day hits us hardest and hurts us most. A well disciplined industrial organisation is the principal weapon of the workers – a weapon to strike with, if need be, or to use as an instrument of peaceful persuasion as occasions arise and circumstances demand.

In amending the Standing Orders the 1924 Congress was accepting the logic of Purcell's argument. The argument was the easier to

[1] For a thorough appraisal of the first Labour Government, see R. W. Lyman, *First Labour Government, 1924* (1957).

accept in view of the strained nature of the relationship between
the T.U.C. and the Government during Labour's brief period
of office. The Government made no attempt to consult the T.U.C.
and Bramley claimed later that he had not had five minutes con-
versation with MacDonald during the latter's premiership.
Bramley suggested that the Labour Party wanted things both
ways. They wanted full integration with the industrial movement
when out of office, but were not interested in consultation when
in power. Individual trade-union leaders had much the same
experience. These feelings found concrete expression in the decision of Bramley and Citrine to end the arrangement whereby
the Research, Publicity and International Departments were run
in conjunction with the Labour Party. The case they presented to
the General Council, in May 1925, for taking this step, was based
on several points, but the crucial one was that the T.U.C.'s sphere
of work was distinct from that of the Labour Party, and that it
therefore needed exclusive control of its own administrative
machinery. Their case was accepted by the Council, and the Joint
Departments were wound up in March 1926, the staff being
divided between the industrial and political wings. Of Henderson's
elaborate scheme for binding the two arms of the movement
together only the National Joint Council remained, and that had
not as yet come near to fulfilling the exalted role which Henderson
had planned for it.

The left-wing interlude in T.U.C. history reached its high
point at the Scarborough Congress of 1925. The Congress was
decidedly militant in tone, and a Communist-inspired resolution
calling for the overthrow of capitalism passed easily. A more
immediately relevant motion called for a further extension of
General Council powers, this time to give the Council direct
executive authority to call affiliated unions out on strike when need
arose. It further instructed affiliated unions to make the necessary
alterations in their rules, in order to permit this transference of
power to the centre. This resolution was not actually sponsored
by the General Council, but Swales in his Presidential Address
made reference to the need for development to take place on these
lines. He stated that he expected the next Congress to be 'ready to
pass in concrete form machinery which establishes the General
Council of the T.U.C. as the central controlling and directing body
of the British Trade Union Movement on all large issues.' Naturally

opinion was divided on so momentous an issue as that raised by the resolution, but Congress did not definitely reject the proposal made. On the suggestion of Bevin the proposal was referred to the General Council, who were authorised to examine it and make recommendations to a special conference of union executives. To some it must have seemed as if the T.U.C. at last stood on the brink of transformation into a federal organisation.

It was not to be. The left-wing interlude ended after Scarborough. Swales was replaced by the moderate Pugh as chairman of the General Council, and Thomas returned to the Council. Bramley was dead before 1925 was out, and Citrine, who shared his viewpoint, had not as yet the authority to adequately replace him. It was not distinctly realised at the time that a fundamental change was taking place, for Hicks, Purcell and Swales all remained on the Council. Nevertheless, a fundamental change there was. Yet the shift in policy in 1924–5, brief though it was and quickly reversed, had one momentous consequence. The General Strike of 1926 would never have occurred, in all probability, but for that brief interlude. It was not merely that the widening of the Council's powers in 1924 gave it the constitutional authority to mobilise the union executives in defence of the Miners. More important was the use made of those powers during the coal crisis of 1925.

4. COAL CRISIS AND GENERAL STRIKE

The request of the Miners' Federation for T.U.C. assistance in July 1925 was the first test of the General Council's newly acquired industrial powers. The Council agreed, as we have seen, to support the Miners and set up a Special Industrial Committee to see how best the support could be rendered. In the event they decided upon an embargo on the movement of coal, and called the executives of the transport unions together to obtain their support for such a policy. The latter agreed and an Embargo Committee was formed, chaired by Hicks, and representing the executive committees of the transport unions involved in rendering assistance. The details of the embargo were worked out and the plan was ready to come into operation at midnight, 31 July, the day the Miners were to be locked out. It was, however, not needed. The Baldwin Government, which had until the last moment refused to subsidise the industry and so remove the pressure on wages, reversed its policy. It announced that a subsidy would be provided until 1 May 1926, and that in the interval a Royal Commission would investigate the condition of the industry. On this basis the coal owners withdrew their lock-out notices, and a stoppage was avoided. It was quite clear that it had been the threat of an embargo which had produced this reversal of policy. It was equally clear that in May 1926, when the subsidy expired, the crisis would return, and that on this occasion the Government would be under a good deal of pressure from Conservative opinion not to surrender a second time to the threat of massive trade union action.

One of the most significant things about the 1925 coal crisis had been the terms on which the General Council had mobilised assistance for the Miners. The emphasis had been on the second of the two elements in the revised Standing Orders. The Miners' platform of no wage reductions, no increase in hours, and the maintenance of national agreements, had been accepted without question, and no pressure had been put on them to modify this platform in the interests of a peaceful settlement. The major emphasis had been upon organising effective industrial action in support of a programme which the Miners were left to themselves to define. Furthermore, the Special Industrial Committee, which had been appointed by the Council to handle the crisis, was retained in being after 31 July. Its function was not, initially, to work out the lines of a permanent settlement for the industry, it was rather to 'apply itself to the task of devising ways and means of consolidating the resistance of the trade union movement should the attack be renewed.'

The Scarborough Congress which followed the July crisis was, however, as we have seen, a turning point. When the Special Industrial Committee met for the first time after the Congress its chairman was Pugh, not Swales, and its membership included J. H. Thomas. These two dominated the Committee from first to last, right up until the day the General Strike commenced. Thomas was not an ardent exponent of the General Council's powers, he was too closely bound up with the Parliamentary Labour Party, but Pugh had always been a supporter of increased T.U.C. influence. However, he construed the role of the General Council to be something quite different from that envisaged by Swales and Hicks, although the latter ultimately came round to his viewpoint. For Pugh it was the first element in the revised Standing Orders that was all-important. He saw the Committee's function as essentially mediatory, not that of a kind of Labour general staff, mobilising the industrial battalions. Under his influence short shrift was made of the Scarborough resolution regarding increased Council powers for conducting industrial warfare. The matter was referred to the Industrial Committee by the General Council in December 1925, but it was decided by the Committee to take no action. Nor indeed was a single preparation made for extended industrial action on behalf of the Miners when the subsidy ended in May. The full General Council itself did nothing in this direction until nearly the end of April. Yet the Committee, wriggle as it did, could not escape the consequences of the decision taken the previous July.

Pugh and Thomas, rightly or wrongly, did not believe that the Miners' three-part programme could be sustained after the subsidy ended. They felt that while it might be possible to preserve the seven-hour day, and the system of national agreements, some concessions would be necessary on wages. Pugh in particular placed his hopes of a settlement on the recommendations of the Royal Commission which Baldwin had appointed, under the chairmanship of Sir Herbert Samuel. This Commission, while outlining schemes for the reorganisation of the coal industry, was quite clear that some wage reductions would be necessary during the transitional period. It would not recommend a further subsidy to cover this period. Pugh, and the majority of the Special Industrial Committee, accepted the Commission's report as 1 reasonable basis for settlement. Yet they were up against the stark fact that the Miners' Federation refused to accept the necessity for wage reductions, and were adamant in insisting upon the three points for which they had stood in 1925. At meetings of the Committee with the Miners' leaders in the spring of 1926, Thomas and Pugh pressed them to give ground. The T.U.C., they were told, could not call a General Strike to enforce a subsidy out of the Government. If there was to be no subsidy how, the Miners were asked, could their wages be maintained without creating massive unemployment in the industry? Were they prepared to accept this massive unemployment and closing of pits as a necessary condition for the maintenance of their wages at the existing level? The Miners' leaders did not evade this issue. On 22 April, when pressed on this question, Smith, the President of the Miners' Federation, replied:

If the Miners retained their position for no reduction of wages, they were going to put upwards of 200,000 men out of work . . . It was a big proposition, but as they told the owners, they had to face it. They were determined that if the country wanted coal, it had to give the men who got it a respectable living.[1]

In the event Thomas and Pugh had to support the Miners, even though they had no real belief in the viability of their position. Their hands were tied by the events of the previous July. The T.U.C. having given its unconditional support to the Miners' three-point programme then, could not withdraw support for the same programme nine months later. It was true that during this interval the Government had greatly improved its bargaining position *vis-à-vis* the T.U.C., by making detailed preparations to maintain the flow of essential supplies in the event of a major industrial crisis, but this could hardly be presented to the movement as a valid reason for withdrawing support from the Miners. So it was that at the end of April the General Council summoned to London the executives of the affiliated unions, and placed before them a scheme for sympathetic action on behalf of the Miners. So little had such action occupied the minds of the Council's leadership that they had left the convening of the Conference to the last moment. Symbolically, the 800 or so delegates were crammed into the Memorial Hall, Farringdon Street, the more commodious Central Hall in Westminster being unavailable at such short notice. The Conference was kept in being for three days while the General Council endlessly pursued with the Government the prospect of a negotiated settlement. Only when it became clear that the chances of such a settlement were remote did the General Council place before the delegates a scheme for co-ordinated action that had been hurriedly improvised by a sub-committee under Purcell's chairmanship. Significantly, the scheme contained two facets, as was made clear to the assembled delegates by chairman Arthur Pugh. The main part was of course concerned with the way in which industrial action was to be

---

[1] The argument that wage levels should be maintained even at the cost of greater unemployment, was unacceptable to the General Council in 1926. Four years later, however, in their evidence to the Macmillan Committee on Finance and Industry in 1930, they argued in precisely these terms: see Chapter 6

mobilised on behalf of the Miners. This time an embargo would not suffice to coerce the Government and coal owners, so that a complete stoppage was planned for the transport, printing, building, iron and steel, electricity and gas industries, although certain workers in special categories were exempted. This was to be the front line; if necessary further industries would be called out in support. The stoppage was to take effect as from midnight, Monday 3 May. The second aspect of the scheme was that the Miners' Federation was to hand over the conduct of the dispute to the General Council. In view of the eventual outcome of the General Strike a lot of controversy was later to develop around this point, but there is no doubt that it was regarded by the General Council as a vital prerequisite for their action in support of the Miners. As we have seen, the Council's leadership had no belief in the possibility of achieving the Miners' three-point programme. With control over the dispute, however, they would be in a position to adopt a more flexible approach. They would, in fact, be able to negotiate a settlement on the Miners' behalf; without wage reductions if possible, but with them if necessary. The second facet of the Council's scheme was thus in effect an escape clause, making provision for an orderly retreat which the leadership felt to be inevitable.

The General Council's blueprint for co-ordinated industrial action was accepted by the union executives on Saturday, 1 May, the mining lock-out commencing the same day. On the following Tuesday the General Strike began. As is well known the response of the movement to the strike call was magnificent, and exceeded all expectation. Nor, during the nine days that the strike lasted, did this initial solidarity and enthusiasm diminish. But it was not enough. It quickly became clear that the preparations made in advance by the Government enabled it to maintain the supply of essential goods and services, and thus hold out against the strikers. The improvised road transport system was decisive. Only rarely did the Government find it necessary to threaten drastic action in order to keep supplies flowing, but where such threats were made, as in the case of the opening of London docks to road transport, they were effective. The dilemma of the General Council was so fundamental that it is almost incredible that so little consideration had been given to it in advance. The issue was what action to take in face of the Government's success in improvising transport and services. To take no action was to admit certain defeat. But to seek to disrupt these improvised arrangements, by vigorous picketing for instance, was openly to challenge the authority of the state. Such a course of action ran the risk of bloodshed, rioting and the transformation of the conflict into something much more than an industrial dispute. While such a development held considerable attraction for the Communists in the movement, it was for the majority of the General Council a prospect to be viewed only with horror. Indeed, it quickly became clear that the principal anxiety of the Council was not so much how to make the stoppage more effective, as how to keep it within bounds. Unofficial initiatives from the localities were distrusted, and a suggestion by Citrine that the trades councils should be made responsible for the conduct of the dispute at local level was rejected. Everything had to be done through the official machinery of the individual unions, or so the Council tried to insist. In fact, of course, local initiative counted for everything in the conduct of the stoppage, but it was exercised in spite of the leadership in Eccleston Square, rather than with its encouragement. The dread of unofficial elements gaining control dominated the policy of the Council.[1]

Given the success of the Government in maintaining essential supplies, given also the repudiation by the Council of a more radical policy in combating this achievement (efforts were made to keep strikers *off* the streets), a stalemate ensued which ensured the defeat of the unions sooner or later. The General Council determined that it should be sooner. A formula for terminating the stoppage was found in the proposals for a settlement put forward by Samuel – the chairman of the late Royal Commission. The proposals were put before the Miners' Federation for their acceptance. The Miners had agreed at the beginning of the dispute to the General Council taking over control, but they interpreted this as meaning that while the General Council would conduct negotiations on their behalf, the final decision as to what was acceptable and what was not should remain with them – an interpretation the General Council did not accept. Since they were not prepared to make any concessions to the owners they rejected the Samuel proposals, which in any case emanated purely from Samuel

[1] For full accounts of the General Strike, see W. H. Crook, *The General Strike* (Chapel Hill 1931) and Julian Symons, *The General Strike* (1957).

himself and had no official standing. Nevertheless, without the Miners' acceptance, the General Council called the strike off, at noon on 12 May. The Miners were thus left to fight alone. The manner in which the strike was called off was as hastily conceived as that in which it had been started nine days earlier. No attempt was made to secure reinstatement for those who had been out, but the Council hoped that all the strikers would be quickly re-employed. However, some employers sought to penalise their workers for supporting the miners, until a massive unofficial demonstration discouraged reprisals by management for the losses suffered during the nine days. Even so, there was some victimisation of strikers. Whatever may be said of the Council's decision to call off the 1926 General Strike, the manner in which the decision was carried out was certain to leave the miners with a sense of betrayal. Not the least unfortunate aspect of the affair was the impression conveyed by the Council that the strike had been ended on the basis of assurances from the Government which would enable the Miners to negotiate an acceptable settlement of their dispute. It was soon apparent that there was no more substance to the Council's explanation of its decision than wish fulfilment. Many members of the General Council did believe that, but for the intransigence of the miners' leaders, the conflict could have been honourably resolved, and they felt they had taken the right course in calling the strike off. In truth, no one – miners' leaders, owners, T.U.C. General Council or the Government – came out of the affair with any credit, except the workers themselves.

5. POST-MORTEM

The collapse of the 1926 General Strike was of course a land-mark in the history of the T.U.C. Immediately it resulted in a severe fall in union membership and morale, but far more than that it meant an urgent need for a reappraisal of the role of Congress and indeed of the movement as a whole. The movement was uniquely fortunate in having two leaders – Bevin and Citrine – of sufficient calibre to carry through such a task. The task of re-appraisal will be the concern of the next chapter, but here it is worth pausing for a moment to reflect upon the significance of the years 1921–6. The case for a thoroughgoing reform of the trade-union movement was very strong in the post-1918 era. As long as the union movement was relatively small-scale, and industrial disputes merely local in character, inter-union squabbles and the unco-ordinated use of the strike weapon did not matter very much. But with close on eight million trade unionists after the war things were different. The General Council was created to bring order into the chaotic union scene, and under the inspiration of Fred Bramley it worked hard during the years 1921–5 to achieve this end. But it failed in almost everything it tried to do. The efforts to increase total trade-union membership provoked an unholy inter-union squabble at the 1923 Congress. Subsequently the Council succeeded in improving the machinery for arbitrating inter-union disputes, but efforts to remove the more fundamental causes of disunity by structural reforms proved to be entirely abortive, as we shall see in the next chapter. The attempt to improve the cohesion of the movement by creating local agencies of Congress, in the shape of the trades councils, had only limited success. The crucial attempt to give the Council power to control and co-ordinate the use of industrial action, although apparently successful in 1924, was shown in 1926 to have been a disastrous failure. Other initiatives, such as the attempt to create an educational system for the movement, proved equally abortive. The group system, which was supposed to have been the means by which the T.U.C. would be integrated fully into the industrial activities of affiliated unions and their federations, never functioned as planned.

It can be argued that all the above are reforms of which the trade-union movement stands in need today. The failure to carry them through in the twenties has often been cited in more recent years as an argument for not making the attempt again. Failure in the twenties resulted from the circumstance that the issue of T.U.C. industrial powers was inextricably bound up with the use of the massive strike weapon, and therefore with left-wing militancy. This was so because the most active exponents of T.U.C. influence were the left-wingers, and it was through them that Bramley worked. We have seen the crisis this produced in 1925–6, when the composition of the Council shifted. The outcome was the disaster of May 1926. The effect of the General Strike was to make it clear that massive industrial action, if it was to succeed, involved a direct challenge to the authority of the state. In refusing to offer this challenge, the General Council was in effect decisively setting its face against the revolutionary elements in the movement. Prior to 1926 the distinction between the Communist and non-Communist Left had to a certain extent been blurred, and both had a common platform of large-scale industrial militancy. After the General Strike the Communists were isolated, for among the trade-union establishment few would again argue in favour of co-ordinated industrial action from the centre. The result was unfortunate from the standpoint of the T.U.C.'s development, for the argument in favour of a transfer of power to the centre had never rested solely, or even mainly, on the need for massive industrial action, yet the one was discredited with the other. The 1926 General Strike thus left the T.U.C. with little room for manœuvre, for any attempt to develop its authority locally, through the trades councils, or nationally through co-ordination of affiliated unions' industrial policy, seemed to correspond with the objectives of the Communists. Nothing, it was felt, ought to be done that would in any way undermine the official leaderships of the individual affiliated unions. In the light of the antagonism to Communism, the *status quo* acquired a new sanctity.

6 Facing the Facts, 1926-31

I. AN END AND A BEGINNING

AFTER the calling off of the General Strike, the General Council was immediately faced with the problem of how to explain its decision to the movement. It was at first proposed to convene a conference of executives during the summer of 1926, but with the Miners' lock-out still continuing, and with the movement bitterly divided over the Council's decision, the conference was postponed with the Miners' agreement. Thus, when the 1926 Congress met at Bournemouth the events of May had still not been debated. The General Council reported to Congress that it intended to postpone an inquest until after the termination of the mining dispute. This was expecting a good deal of restraint from Congress delegates, and the decision was challenged by Jack Tanner of the Amalgamated Engineering Union. Tanner raised an important point. The General Council, he argued, was elected by Congress and was responsible to it; it had no right to withhold information or prevent discussion of so vital an issue. President Pugh did not accept Tanner's interpretation:

The Congress had no power, and has conferred no power, upon the General Council to call a National Strike. . . . So far as the General Council had powers in relation to the strike it could only have those powers in consultation with the authorities of the unions which would be affected and the measure of the General Council's authority was conferred upon it by the Executives of the Trade Unions which met previous to the National Strike. Therefore, the General Council feel that that authority having been given by the Executives, it is to the Executives they must make their report.

The delegates accepted Pugh's line on the matter, but the issue revealed the anomalous position of Congress. It elected the General Council, but had no power to delegate authority to it – for this the Council had to go outside the regularly constituted Congress and convene a special conference of union executives. This cumbersome procedure has continued to the present time, and is a striking testimony to the strength of the doctrine of individual union autonomy, whereby the central committee requires the permission of the governing body of each individual union before it can claim to commit the movement to any line of action. Any hope of reconstituting Congress on federal lines, with the General Council functioning as an Executive Committee, was buried after 1926 along with the General Strike weapon.

Although the General Council's handling of the mining dispute was not debated at Bournemouth the bitterness of feeling on this issue could not be completely suppressed. An emergency resolution calling for maximum financial assistance for the miners, who were still locked out, produced an uproar. The trouble arose from the fact that the President had called upon John Bromley, secretary of the Locomotivemen, to second the resolution. Bromley had been severely critical of the Miners' Federation, and his appointment to second the resolution was regarded by the latter as an insult. The resultant turmoil was such that the President had to adjourn Congress and the delegates left the hall, many singing the Red Flag. This exhibition of militancy was, however, misleading. The mood of the previous Scarborough Congress had vanished. When A. G. Tomkins, of the left-wing Furnishing Trades Association, reopened the question of a further extension of the Council's powers to co-ordinate industrial action he met with a cool reception. Bevin was opposed, and so was Clynes. As the latter said:

The movement is in a reflective mood. It finds itself full of contemplation on the meaning and the lessons of the unprecedented adventure into which the trade union movement entered at the beginning of May.

In effect the matter was closed. In another direction, however, the Left appeared to score a success. Another resolution, also moved by Tomkins, instructed the General Council to call conferences of the trade groups of the Congress in order to arrange for the merging of the separate unions within these groups into industrial unions. This was the second great radical cause of the twenties, industrial unionism, and the passage of the resolution through Congress in 1926 indicated it still had some life in it. Some life, but not much, for a year later the General Council produced its 'authoritative report' on trade-union structure.

Citrine was elected Secretary of the T.U.C. at the Bournemouth Congress, a post he was to hold until after the Second World War. He had been Acting Secretary since Bramley's death in 1925. At thirty-nine he was the youngest Secretary in the history of Congress. His capacity was quickly put to the test, for with the ending of the mining lock-out in December 1926, the time had at last arrived for the inquest into the events of May. The postponed Conference of Executives met in January 1927 at the Central Hall, Westminster. The 1,200 delegates had before them two reports, one from the General Council, the other from the Miners Federation. The General Council claimed that its behaviour had been consistent, and that the shambles had resulted from the fact that the Miners had gone back on their undertaking to hand over control of negotiations to the Council. Whatever the merits of this argument, there was no doubt that Citrine had prepared the Council's case with characteristic thoroughness and efficiency, and the Conference accepted it by a large majority. The interval of eight months since the end of the strike clearly helped, for feelings had died down and the inquest took place in a relatively calm atmosphere.

One consequence of the failure of the General Strike kept the Council much preoccupied during the course of 1927. The massive Conservative majority in the House of Commons was not to be denied its pound of flesh, and this it took in the form of the Trade Disputes and Trade Union Bill. This outlawed general and sympathetic strikes, curbed the unions' right to picket, and introduced the principle of contracting in where the political levy to the Labour Party was concerned. It has been described, rightly, as an irresponsible and vindictive piece of class legislation.[1] The General Council made strenuous efforts to oppose the passage of the Bill into law. It called a special conference of executives on the subject, in April 1927, and this was followed by local conferences and demonstrations during the summer months. All was, however, predictably to no avail, and the Bill passed duly through its stages. It was resented by the Labour Movement more than any other piece of legislation passed this century, less because of its content than because of the vindictiveness that was its inspiration. Its repeal was high among the priorities of the first majority Labour Government, elected in 1945.

[1] See Crook, *The General Strike*, p. 481.

D

The Congress that met in Edinburgh in the autumn of 1927 had politics very much on its mind. The position of the unions in industry had been badly damaged by the General Strike and in addition they were now faced with punitive Government legislation. It was no surprise, therefore, when George Hicks, in his Presidential speech, referred to the immediate task of the movement as being the return of a Labour Government at the next general election. Although, with the experience of 1924 in mind, he was careful to stress that a Labour Government's programme 'should be well thought out beforehand and well understood'. Ironically, however, in view of these political preoccupations, the Edinburgh Congress marked the beginning of an attempt by the industrial wing to seek its own economic salvation, irrespective of the state of play at Westminster. The starting point for this attempt was also contained in Hicks' opening Presidential address. In his speech he referred to the need for a 'direct exchange of practical views between representatives of the great organised bodies who have responsibility for the conduct of industry', meaning the General Council on one side and the Federation of British Industries and the National Confederation of Employers' Organisations on the other. Since the end of the General Strike there had been a lot of talk about the need for greater harmony in industrial relations. In December 1926, for example, the *Westminster Gazette* had held an 'Industrial Peace Banquet'. While the vagueness of such liberal sentiments rather exasperated the T.U.C. leadership, they did indicate that opinion in the country was by no means united behind the heavy-handed reactionaries in the House of Commons. Many employers were in favour of a more positive approach to industrial relations, and made this known to their opposite numbers in the unions. This then was the background to the idea thrown out by Hicks. The idea was developed further in the long awaited report on trade union organisation and structure, which the General Council presented to the Edinburgh Congress. The Report made the following observation:

The extent to which the Confederation of Employers' Organisations controls questions of general policy, in the opinion of the General Council, points to the necessity for centralised negotiations to deal with general questions for the whole movement. The General Council therefore recommends that the necessary co-ordination should be in the hands of the T.U.C. through the medium of the General Council.

In a sense this line of reasoning represented the continuation of labour policy whereby trade-union organisation was seen as marching in step with developments in capitalist industry, centralisation and consolidation on the one side being met by similar developments on the other. The difference was that trade-union leaders no longer envisaged the concentration of labour's industrial power as a means whereby concessions could be extracted from capitalism by force. They counted on both sides of industry shrinking in the future from such a policy of confrontation. They counted on the employers, like themselves, being desirous of finding a way out of the impasse. Furthermore it was not implied in the Report that centralised negotiations on general issues would necessitate any transfer of powers to the General Council. It was in any case hardly an opportune moment for the consideration of such an issue. Congress therefore allowed this aspect of the Report to pass without debate. Hicks's 'direct exchange of practical views' between the two sides of industry was still a merely academic question in 1927.

The main concern of the Report was with the structure of affiliated unions, and its conclusion in this respect produced plenty of discussion. The Report, it will be remembered, grew out of a resolution passed at the Southport Congress of 1922, but the Organisation Committee of the T.U.C. which produced the final document took as its terms of reference a resolution passed at Hull in 1924. This had been a composite resolution instructing the General Council both to prepare a scheme for the reorganisation of the movement on the basis of industrial unionism, and to work for a reduction in the number of unions by fostering amalgamations. Industrial unionism was one of the great radical causes of early twentieth-century unionism. It drew its support from left-wing elements, and from those unions, irrespective of ideology, already constituted on an industrial basis. The grouping system devised in 1921 to govern elections to the General Council represented an aspiration towards industrial unionism. This was still recognised in 1926, when, as we saw, Tomkins's resolution on industrial unionism was approved by Congress. The 1927 Report ended such aspirations, almost as completely as the General

Strike ended the movement for a transfer of power to the centre. It stated:

After very careful consideration of the problem the General Council has been forced to the conclusion that as it is impossible to define any fixed boundaries of industry, it is impracticable to formulate a scheme of 'organisation by industry' that can be made applicable to all industries.

Ostensibly the chief argument used to defend this point of view was that technological change resulted in shifting boundaries that made impossible the drawing of clear-cut demarcation lines between one industry and the next. The real point, however, was that in practical terms industrial unionism was ruled out because it would mean the dismembering of the General Unions, which the latter would never agree to. This was not of course spelt out in so many terms, but the General Council made clear its view that the only way forward was to accept the existing mixed structure of the movement (with craft, general and industrial unions) and to seek to improve its functioning by piecemeal mergers and joint working arrangements.

This pragmatic but uninspiring conclusion was not welcome to the Left and Tanner of the A.E.U. moved the reference back, supported by a delegate of the Miners. Tanner did not accept the claim that it was impractical to decide the boundaries between industries, and he cited foreign experience in support of his argument. Of course there would be ragged edges, but this did not justify the General Council in ruling out a definite plan as a basis for organisation. Tanner was opposed, significantly, by representatives of the two big general unions – Dukes for the National Union of General and Municipal Workers and Bevin for the Transport and General Workers Union. Bevin, incidentally, was a member of the Organisation Committee. Perhaps the most effective speech, however, was made by Walkden of the Railway Clerks, who was the Organisation Committee chairman. Walkden made play of the fact that 'expert witnesses from the unions could not define their own industries', and he cited the evidence of the Miners' Federation as an example. When the vote was taken the reference back was narrowly lost by 2,062,000 votes to 1,809,000. The defeat proved, however, to be conclusive, for the 1927 Report came to be accepted as an authoritative refutation of the case for industrial unionism.

The most effective section of the Report was that which dealt with the efforts of the General Council since 1923 to promote amalgamations among affiliated unions. The Council had convened amalgamation conferences in the metal trade, textiles, printing, the post office, insurance, dyeing and bleaching, distribution, leather and building. Yet at the time of the Edinburgh Congress it could record but one success. This was achieved in dyeing and bleaching, where a new society came into existence on 1 January 1927. The Council pointed out in the Report 'that however desirous it may be to achieve amalgamations amongst its constituent unions, the real driving force must come from the unions themselves, and no efforts which the Council may make can accomplish their object if they are met in a reluctant spirit'. One of the problems was that while the executive committees of individual unions could often be brought to agree to a draft scheme, they failed to secure the necessary support from the rank and file owing to inadequate communications within the unions concerned. The rank and file were not given a lead nor were they adequately informed. The Council's recommendations for the future put the responsibility firmly on the shoulders of individual unions. It proposed that each affiliated union should consider its attitude, and declare to the General Council in writing, firstly whether it was prepared to participate in amalgamation negotiations, secondly whether it was prepared to agree to joint working arrangements, and thirdly with which unions it would pursue either or both of the above courses. It was no doubt in part the realism of this section of the Report which influenced Congress in accepting its wider conclusion with regard to industrial unionism.

There is one final aspect of the 1927 Organisation Report which deserves consideration, for this, like the industrial union issue, aroused a good deal of controversy at the time and constitutes something of a turning point in T.U.C. development. One of the most successful General Council initiatives since 1921 had been its attention to the position of the Trades Councils. We saw how a Consultative Committee had been set up in 1924, and since that time much had been done to improve the Councils' effectiveness as local organs of the movement. The drive, however, had come from the full-time officers of Congress, Bramley, Citrine, and Tewson, and the elected Council members were fearful lest the Trades Councils should interfere with the autonomy of affiliated unions. During the coal crisis of 1925–6 they had been strictly prohibited from acting as more than local information bureaux. After the General Strike the problem took on an explicitly ideological form, as the General Council tightened up its attitude towards revolutionary elements in the movement. The Trades Councils, as the well-established stamping ground of the extreme Left, were the first to feel the impact of this development, and the Organisation Committee reported to Congress that the General Council had decided to refuse recognition to any Trades Council that was in any way associated with the National Minority Movement (a Communist front organisation in the trade union movement, founded in 1924). Communists and their sympathisers among the Congress delegates challenged the Council's decision and a long discussion ensued. It was clear, however, that the trade-union leadership had set its face against the Communist Party, and those bodies in the movement which were demonstrably acting under the latter's political direction. As Herbert Smith remarked, 'I can see no difference between the Minority Movement and Communism; they get their orders from Moscow in each case'.

The reaction against Communism, manifest at the 1927 Congress, owed much to the abuse showered by Communists upon General Council leaders in the aftermath of the General Strike. More profoundly, however, as we have seen, the strike had the effect of awakening the leadership to the irreconcilable nature of the gulf that separated revolutionary from non-revolutionary, Communist from non-Communist. Before 1926 the borderline was blurred; after 1926 Citrine and other T.U.C. leaders made it explicit. This was revealed at the 1927 Congress not only with respect to the Trades Councils, but in other decisions that were taken. For instance, since 1924 the T.U.C. had been distinguished from other affiliated members of the International Federation of Trades Unions by its efforts on behalf of international trade-union unity. This meant, in practice, the admission of the Russian union movement into the Federation. Fred Bramley and Alf Purcell, in particular, had spared no efforts in order to achieve this goal, despite the obstinate resistance of Continental unionists, more experienced than the British in Communist methods of subversion. Purcell became completely distrusted by the European leaders as a 'Moscow manœuvrer'. The T.U.C. had set up a special Joint Advisory Council with the Russian movement in 1925, the object of which was to work for the admission of the Russians into the Federation. Relationships on the Council became very strained, however, after the General Strike, and at the 1927 Congress the General Council proposed that its existence be terminated. The proposal was accepted. A much less important decision taken at Edinburgh operated in the same direction. Since 1923 the General Council had co-operated, on paper at any rate, with the National Unemployed Workers' Committee Movement, a body largely dominated by Communists. In 1927 the Council's link with this organisation was also severed.

2. NEW HORIZONS

The 1927 Congress marked an end and a beginning. An end to aspirations for the radical transformation of the structure of the movement, and an end to the loose ideological environment that had characterised the early days of the General Council. Henceforward the anti-Communist basis of the British movement was to be made more and more explicit. The beginning was the suggestion thrown out by Hicks, that aimed at bringing the General Council into contact with the leaders of British industry. In October 1927 the suggestion met with a negative response from the National Confederation of Employers' Organisations, but in the following month the General Council received a letter from a group of influential employers led by Sir Alfred Mond (the chemical magnate), inviting participation in a series of discussions covering general issues affecting industry. The General Council agreed to a preliminary meeting, which was duly held on 12 January 1928, at Burlington House in London. The Council approached this new development with a good deal of caution. In the first place the Mond group of employers had no official standing, unlike the Confederation, and it was not clear what the General Council stood to gain from engaging in discussions with such a body. Secondly, discussion with Mond and his associates raised ideological problems. The Council was sensitive to charges by the Left that it was abandoning its belief in the ultimate transformation of society on socialist lines, and was, by its association with Mond, tacitly accepting the existing system of industrial ownership.

At the opening conference several Council members made it

clear to the employers that while they were interested in discussing how progress could be made within the existing capitalist order, this must not be taken to imply any sacrifice of ultimate socialist objectives, to be achieved constitutionally through the political action of the Labour Party. It was, however, noticeable that the two most outstanding T.U.C. leaders, Citrine and Bevin, were concerned less with these ideological reservations than with the practical advantages that might be gained from the talks. What interested Bevin was the scope of the discussions. In the ordinary course of relations with employers unionists continually found that discussion of anything beyond purely wage and hour questions tended to be ruled out of order by employers, as pertaining to managerial functions. Bevin therefore insisted that if discussions were to be of value nothing associated with the economic side of industry ought to be ruled out. There must be no bogey about managerial functions. He asked for a clear ruling on this point, and Mond was able to satisfy him that the talks would be all-embracing. Citrine's speech was the highlight of the first conference. He appreciated only too well the immaturity of the Labour Movement, its difficulty in moving beyond well-worn propagandist slogans to consider the complexities of modern industrial society:

I am one of those people who have talked in my time as vehemently and indignantly about the evils of capitalism . . . as anyone who has stood on Labour platforms, but I recognise that a time must come in the history of the industrial movement of this country when it tries to translate into practical achievement some of the shibboleths and slogans it has uttered from Labour platforms. It may be that in the translation of these utterances we shall find there is not quite so great a clash of principle, on certain things at least, as some of us have thought.

I can see no joy to the workers of this country in an early collapse of the industrial system. I believe the workers of this country are compelled to apply themselves to getting a higher standard of living under the present system without any prejudice to their conception of what the future may hold. I believe this conference, if rightly guided, will enable us to get a long way along that road.

At the end of this speech Citrine struck a different note:

I want to say that if these negotiations fail through a lack of faith or confidence on anyone's part I do not know how soon we are going to start again. There are two courses, and we are at the turning. If we fail to achieve advancement and a better standard of life for our people, there is another way that many advocates will try to induce Labour to take, and all of us in our deliberations should not overlook our responsibility in trying to choose the right course.

It was a warning that recalcitrant employer attitudes would drive the unions into the arms of the extremists.

After the Burlington House Conference the General Council decided by a majority of eighteen to six to pursue the talks with the Mond Group. The decision was opposed by left-wingers, Cook and Swales, the former later carrying his opposition to the lengths of producing a pamphlet entitled *Mond Moonshine*. The cogent arguments of Bevin, Citrine and Pugh were, however, decisive in carrying the Council forward on its new path. A sub-committee was appointed, including the above three names, to meet with a similar sub-committee drawn from the employers' side, and meetings of the two bodies continued at weekly intervals throughout the first half of 1928. The talks ranged over a wide field, memoranda were prepared and adopted, and an Interim Joint Report was adopted unanimously. The Report dealt with Government monetary policy and its impact upon industry, trade union recognition, victimisation, the establishment of a National Industrial Council, conciliation of industrial disputes, and rationalisation in industry. The Report was submitted to a second full conference of the General Council and the Mond Group in July 1928. It was accepted with only one dissentient, A. J. Cook, who made the amusing assertion that the acceptance of the Report by the Labour Movement indicated it had 'lost its soul for a mess of indigestible pottage!' Cook was not, however, without support in the wider movement, for the participation of the Council in the talks had been a controversial issue from the beginning. At the 1928 Swansea Congress the General Council would be on trial to justify the action it had taken.

The debate on the Mond Conferences at Swansea lasted an entire day, and it made the 1928 Congress one of the most memorable of the inter-war period. Citrine opened for the General Council, Clynes and Thomas gave support during the debate, and Bevin wound the case up. By the overwhelming majority of 3,075,000 votes to 566,000 the delegates voted to continue the

talks. The combination of Citrine and Bevin was the most
brilliant in the history of the movement, and it was one to which the
opposition had no answer. But the opposition was in any case
weak because of the post 1926 climate of opinion. Both Hicks and
Swales opposed the continuance of the talks, Hicks perhaps
surprisingly in view of his 1927 initiative. Both had played a large
part in the leftward shift in Congress policy during the mid-
twenties, and they were sensitive now to charges that the General
Council was collaborating with the capitalists. But neither could
afford to base his opposition now upon a simple anti-capitalist
argument, for this was to risk identification with the Communists.
They relied therefore upon the weak arguments that the Council
was exceeding its powers, and that the employers' group was
unofficial and unrepresentative. The straightforward left-wing
view was put by Cook and Tomkins, but the former spoke merely
as an individual, for the Miners supported the General Council,
and the latter represented only the small Furnishing Trades
Association. The debate thus provided one more illustration of the
isolation of the Left in the post-1926 situation. As if to ram
the point home further the 1928 Congress authorised
the General Council to conduct a full enquiry into 'disruptive' (meaning Communist) elements and activities in the
movement.

It would, however, be less than just to present the leadership
of Bevin and Citrine in terms of a victory for the Right over the
Left, because it was precisely from such general labels and slogans
that they were seeking to rescue the movement. They were looking
for a constructive policy which the trade unions could pursue in
the present, rather than merely confining themselves to defending
wages and hours, until such time as a Labour majority at Westminster would remove all their problems and establish Socialism.
Citrine was not afraid to spell this out to the movement in concrete terms. In the General Council Report to the 1928 Congress
it was pointed out that given the fact that the movement rejected
revolution, it was left with the alternatives of either sitting back
and letting the employers get on with the job of management,
what Citrine called on another occasion 'standing at a distance and
calling names', or involving itself positively in the formation of
economic policy and thereby seeking to improve material standards
in the here and now. This was the justification for the Mond–

Turner talks.[1] Two very important consequences followed from Citrine's and Bevin's approach, consequences which in their beneficial effects compensated to some extent for the lost momentum towards centralisation and structural reorganisation. The first was that if the movement was to demand a larger share in the determination of economic policy, it would have to educate itself. Slogans and propaganda were no longer enough. The point was well put by Bevin in his speech at the 1928 Congress:

I look forward to the time when the General Council will be coming and laying before this great parliament of its own creation annual reports on the discussion of great economic problems, trying to direct your attention on lines of analysis, lines of investigation and not mere debating points blown by the wind. Thus and thus only will the movement be really intelligently dealing with the real economic problems of our times.

The second point, which Bevin also made during the debate, was that the industrial movement needed to function independently of the political arm, even while subscribing to the latter's long-term objectives. It had to kill once for all the notion that contact with industrial leaders was somehow incompatible with its wider Socialist objectives. Unlike political parties trade unions are always 'in office' and their job is to make the very best of the situation as it exists at the present time. This meant involvement in industry, capitalist industry. Such involvement need not mean loss of independence; the guarantee of independence was the educational process referred to above, which would equip labour leaders to discuss the whole range of economic problems on an equal footing with the capitalists. A theme that constantly recurs in the speeches of Bevin and Citrine is their attention to labour's inferiority complex, the feeling 'that labour is going to get the worst of the deal in entering into discussions with the employers'. They wanted the unions to have the confidence in themselves to claim to discuss with government and employers all the major economic problems that affected the well-being of workers, rather than to take refuge behind ill-defined slogans devoid of practical content. Not long after the Swansea Congress the General Council created a new sub-committee, the Economic Committee. Although the credit for its

[1] So called because Sir Alfred Mond (later Lord Melchett) was leader of the employers' group, while Ben Turner was General Council chairman for 1927–8.

formation belongs to the head of the T.U.C. Research Department, W. Milne-Bailey, the Committee reflected the new direction given to the T.U.C. leadership by Bevin and Citrine. In the period after 1928 it was to become what the Joint Defence Committee had been before 1925 – the focus of the Council's activities. The difference between the names of the two committees alone reflects the shift in emphasis that had taken place.

The discussions with the Mond Group were resumed after the Swansea Congress, and a detailed investigation was made by the two sub-committees into the problem of unemployment. To some extent, however, interest was shifting on to another plain. It had always been the hope of the T.U.C. leaders, and indeed of the Mond Group also, that their informal discussions would ultimately lead to a more permanent arrangement, in which the T.U.C. would engage in discussions with the regular employer organisations – the N.C.E.O. and the F.B.I. At the very first meeting with the Mond Group in January 1928 Citrine had spoken of the need to create a National Economic Council, able to speak authoritatively for the whole of industry, and the creation of such a body was one of the issues discussed at subsequent meetings. Mond himself was an enthusiastic supporter of the idea. The assumption behind the idea of an Economic Council was that the trade unions and employers, whatever their conflicts, shared a common interest in industrial prosperity. Further, that they, rather than the government of the day, were in the best position to determine where the true interest of industry lay. An instance of the latter point occurred with respect to monetary matters, where it could be argued that Government policy was having detrimental effects upon the level of industrial activity. Mond took this view. He had opposed the return to the Gold Standard in 1925 and the deflationary policy that it entailed. It had been on his initiative that the matter had been brought up for discussion in the Mond–Turner conversations. Hitherto trade unionists had given little serious thought to the impact of monetary policy on wage and employment levels, so that their discussion of the problem with the Mond Group proved extremely illuminating. An agreed statement on the matter was incorporated in the Joint Interim Report, which included a demand for a full Government inquiry into credit policy. Here then was one issue where industry as a whole might have a common interest in pressing a particular policy upon the state.

Similarly, with regard to industrial disputes. The Government's handling of the 1926 coal crisis did not inspire confidence either among unionists or among the more progressive employers. Perhaps such problems as those of the coal industry would be better handled if the Government was obliged to take advice from an authoritative body representing the two sides of industry. So at any rate Mond argued, and there were those on the General Council who were prepared to agree with him.

The proposal to set up a National Industrial Council representative of the T.U.C. on one side and the N.C.E.O. and F.B.I. on the other was embodied in the Joint Interim Report agreed upon in July 1928. Subsequently the Report had been referred to the two employers' organisations for their consideration. No reply was, however, forthcoming until February 1929, when the F.B.I. and N.C.E.O. notified the T.U.C. and the Mond Group that they were unable to accept the Report. The reason given was that the two employers' organisations had no authority to lay down policy for their constituent members, and could not therefore participate in a National Council, nor could they endorse the various policy recommendations contained in the Report. It appeared that in practice the F.B.I. and the N.C.E.O. had even less authority over their constituents than did the T.U.C. Behind these constitutional objections there was also the fact that the majority of employers were a good deal less progressive in viewpoint than those who comprised the Mond Group. The F.B.I. and N.C.E.O., however, while rejecting the Interim Report, did intimate that they would be prepared to engage in consultations with the T.U.C. The consultations, however, would have to be between the T.U.C. and *either* the F.B.I. *or* the N.C.E.O., but not both together, for the functions of each were regarded as being quite distinct.[1] Furthermore, there was to be no question of a wide-ranging, planned agenda, such as had characterised talks with the Mond Group. Discussions were to be on merely individual issues, as they arose.

The General Council regarded the reply of the N.C.E.O. and F.B.I. as a severe setback. The discussions with the Mond Group had been highly valued, and the T.U.C. leaders were reluctant to abandon them for the much more limited type of consultation approved by the two employers' organisations. Furthermore, they

[1] The F.B.I. dealt with general economic issues affecting industry, while the N.C.E.O. was confined to labour matters.

were disturbed by the rejection of the Joint Interim Report, because it implied a refusal to subscribe to the statements in favour of trade union recognition, and against victimisation, which had constituted an important part of the Report. The biggest blow, however, was the setback to the notion of a National Industrial Council, which had become by 1929 the main objective towards which the T.U.C. and the Mond Group were working. Nevertheless both the General Council and the Mond Group felt that the offer of consultation by the employers' federations should be taken up, in the hope that out of such talks something like an Industrial Council might ultimately emerge. The full General Council and the Mond Group met, for what proved to be the last time, in March 1929, when a report on unemployment was adopted. The Conference was then adjourned pending the result of developments with the N.C.E.O. and the F.B.I. The following month the General Council met representatives from the latter bodies at the Hotel Metropole in London, and began to hammer out a satisfactory basis for future consultations.

The preliminary negotiations with the two employers' federations dragged on throughout the remainder of 1929, with the General Council trying to work towards a relationship similar to that with the Mond Group, while the N.C.E.O. and F.B.I. clung to the idea of limited consultations on the basis of specific issues. The employers' insistence on the division of functions between their two federations, and the resultant necessity for separate consultations with the T.U.C., was felt by the General Council to be simply a device for restricting the range of discussions, in that either of the two federations could stall on an awkward issue by proclaiming that it was beyond its terms of reference. The problem was further complicated by the advent of a Labour Government following the general election in May 1929. Bevin in particular suspected that the N.C.E.O. was worried about possible legislation relating to labour matters which the new Government might introduce, and that it saw consultations with the T.U.C. chiefly as a form of insurance against undesired legislation. Nevertheless, in December 1929 agreement was finally reached on a basis for future consultations. The progress made by the General Council since the previous February concerned the spirit more than the precise manner in which consultations were to be organised. They got the employers to agree to a wide range of *possible* topics for discussion, but the principle of division of function between the F.B.I. and N.C.E.O. remained. It was agreed that the employers would set up an 'allocation committee', to which any particular General Council proposal for consultation would be referred; the Committee would then decide whether the F.B.I. or the N.C.E.O. was the appropriate body to deal with the matter. This machinery was agreed upon at a joint conference at the Metropole on 19 December. The mood of the meeting, surprisingly perhaps, was mainly one of self-congratulation and optimism. Will Thorne, a General Council member, said he 'felt that they were like one large family', and John Beard, the Council chairman, felt moved to refer to his pride in being British. Nor did A. J. Cook indulge in his usual anti-capitalist tirade, having been converted to support of the Council's policy earlier in the year. Indeed, Cook was delegated to move the acceptance of the joint report. Not all, however, on the unions' side were happy in this atmosphere. Perhaps it was the mood of self-satisfaction which prompted Bevin (otherwise silent) to move that the parties involved in the Mond–Turner conferences be remembered, for without the unofficial conferences the present meeting would never have taken place. But it was John Bromley who really struck a discordant note. It was all very well to sit around the table and talk goodwill, but how were individual employers behaving in industry?

He appealed to everyone present to see that co-operation which had been spoken of at the conference should be actually carried out in science and in fact.

Bromley's intervention was timely, for while a basis had been established for contact with the F.B.I. and N.C.E.O., it remained to be seen how far such contact could be turned to the concrete advantage of labour.

While these developments had been under way the Annual Congress of 1929, held at Belfast, had come and gone. Ben Tillett, the veteran leader of the 1889 dock strike, was the year's President. His address reflected fully the wide-ranging economic interests which the Council had acquired as a result of the Mond–Turner talks. He spoke of government financial policy, of the need for rationalisation and the use of scientific methods in British industry, and of the possibility of the British Commonwealth being organised 'as an economic unit', comparable to the U.S.A. It was significant

that these were the issues highlighted by Tillett, and not the fact
that a Labour Government was in office. The trade union leaders
of the late twenties, struck by the example of America, no longer
saw the material livelihood of the workers as a mainly *political*
problem. They were already thinking more in terms of economic
growth than of redistribution. Of course, this was a trend that was
noticeable chiefly among the leadership of the movement, and the
limited perspective of some elements in the unions was amusingly
illustrated at the 1929 Congress, when the Musicians' Union
moved a resolution asking for legislation against talking motion
pictures. As a delegate said, 'our friends might as well try and
push back the tide as try to push back the progress of the Talkies'.
The resolution was lost. The most important item the Congress
had to discuss was the General Council's report into the disruptive
tactics of the Communists within the movement. The report arose
as we saw, out of a decision to hold an enquiry into 'disruption',
taken the previous year at Swansea. Citrine did the job with
characteristic thoroughness. The degree of Communist influence
revealed by the enquiry was not in fact alarming, but the report
had an educational value in that it illuminated the ways in which
Communist infiltration was accomplished, as for instance in the
deliberate use of non-Communist left-wingers as front men for
the furtherance of Communist Party policies. The extent to which
these policies were derived from Moscow was also established.
Furthermore, the report sought to identify those apparently
independent organisations, such as the League against Imperialism, which were in fact Communist-controlled. When the report
was debated an attempt was made by some pro-Communist
delegates to assert the integrity of these organisations, but Citrine
was able to satisfy Congress that his interpretation was the most
accurate. Citrine was determined that the movement should face
up to the real nature of Communism, and set its face against it.
This was the purpose of the 1929 Report.

In its report to the 1929 Congress the General Council had
drawn attention to its negotiations with the F.B.I. and the
N.C.E.O., and subsequently, as we saw, in December 1929
agreement was reached with these bodies on consultative machinery. The machinery was quickly activated, for in February 1930
the F.B.I. came forward with proposals for talks on two topics.
The first concerned the nature of the evidence to be submitted by

the two bodies to the Macmillan Committee on Finance and Industry. This Committee had been appointed by the Labour Government, and included Ernest Bevin among its members. The Mond–Turner Conference had called for an investigation into credit policy in 1928, and this no doubt had influenced the Government in setting up the Committee. In the event the General Council prepared its evidence independently of the F.B.I. but some limited consultation between the two bodies did take place. The T.U.C. evidence to the Committee was given in May 1930. In its sophistication and grasp of the complexities of the economic situation it revealed the lasting impact of the Mond–Turner talks upon T.U.C. thinking. The detailed argument behind the General Council's evidence need not concern us, but its general direction is important, especially in the light of later events. The Council was concerned to rule out wage cutting as a solution to Britain's economic problems. Such a policy had not brought relief to the depressed British coal industry, because any competitive advantage gained by a lowering of domestic wage levels was quickly lost when foreign competitors followed suit. The T.U.C. statement went on:

If the choice had to be made, we would prefer the alternative of unemployment to that of unemployment eliminated at the cost of a degradation in the standard of living of the workers. We are confident that, given international action (to raise prices), and given also the re-organisation of our basic industries, such a situation would only be temporary. We are quite convinced that the right policy is to concentrate upon raising the efficiency of labour, and not upon reducing the purchasing power of the wage earners, so intensifying the evil. This very question of the efficiency of labour is one that is left entirely out of account by those who talk of British wage rates being high. They forget American wage rates. They forget that international comparisons of wages are meaningless without a comparison of wage costs.

The maintenance of wage levels was thus an absolute priority in the Council's policy, and it was even prepared to envisage devaluation rather than concur in any attempt to lower living standards. This was made clear in a public statement by the General Council at the time when the report of the Macmillan Committee was published in 1931. Furthermore Bevin, as a member of the Committee, wrote an addendum to its report in which he dissented from the rest of the Committee in refusing to rule out the possibility of devaluation.

The second issue which the F.B.I. wished to explore with the T.U.C. was the possibility of the two sides of industry agreeing upon a common policy on Commonwealth matters. The particular interest of the F.B.I. was in the development of the Commonwealth as an economic unit, a possibility to which, as we have seen, Tillett had referred at the 1929 Congress. At a joint T.U.C./ F.B.I. meeting in May 1930, the employers put forward proposals recommending the creation of an Imperial Economic Conference and a permanent Imperial Economic Secretariat. The General Council was in favour of this idea of Commonwealth economic machinery, and agreed to make representations to the Government, together with the F.B.I., in order to achieve this end. The issue was a live one, as an Imperial Conference was due to meet at the end of the year. While the General Council favoured the creation of machinery for Commonwealth economic co-operation, it was wary of proposals to develop an Empire economic bloc by means of tariff arrangements. The labour movement was traditionally committed to free trade, and there was likely to be a good deal of opposition to any radical departure from this standpoint. The Commonwealth issue was the most important subject for debate at the 1930 Nottingham Congress, where Ernest Bevin presented the General Council's economic report and carried the day in favour of Commonwealth economic co-operation. The issue of free trade versus protection was, however, left open. The Council's support for Commonwealth co-operation left it wide open to attack from the Left, for the charge of imperialism was only too easy to make, but Congress delegates were prepared to support the Council's line because it had at least the merit of being constructive. As Cramp of the Railwaymen said: 'What are the alternatives? I have not heard any put up in this Congress. . . . Those who put forward those glib phrases without any explanation are doing so because they are too tired to think'.

3. UNIONISTS AND POLITICIANS – THE CONFRONTATION OF 1931

One consequence of the development in T.U.C. policy since 1926 was to strain its relationship to the Labour Party, and in particular to the Labour Government formed in June 1929. Relations had not been easy during the period of the first Labour Government, in 1924, but various factors made things even more difficult after 1929. As a recent writer on the second Labour Government has pointed out, Labour Party politicians lacked a constructive policy for dealing with the immediate economic situation; their thought was dominated by the long-term objective of transforming society on socialist lines, but this objective offered no guidance as to what policies ought to be pursued in the immediate situation.[1] The immediate situation was critical, for whereas unemployment had certainly been bad when the Government took office, it quickly became very much worse as a world-wide depression developed following the Wall Street crash in the autumn of 1929. The lack of any policy for the short-term forced the Labour Ministers into dependence upon orthodox views as to what were the appropriate policies to be pursued. In contrast to the Labour Party the T.U.C. had, as we have seen, made a striking attempt to face up to current economic problems. Consequently, while it was, like other elements in the community, unable to offer any ready-made solution to the problem of depression, it was sure of itself on certain points, as the evidence submitted to the Macmillan Committee made abundantly clear. From the beginning the T.U.C. leadership found itself in conflict with MacDonald's ministry. The focus of the conflict was the question of Unemployment Insurance. The T.U.C. had informed the Macmillan Committee that the maintenance of wage levels was an absolute priority so far as it was concerned, to be obtained if necessary at the cost of a higher rate of unemployment than would otherwise have existed. From this standpoint Unemployment Insurance assumed a vital significance. In the first place, if one was prepared to accept, in the short run at any rate, a high level of unemployment, the least that could be done was to ensure a decent level of maintenance for those out of work, to be secured through adequate insurance benefits. But secondly, the preservation of wage levels was in itself dependent upon adequate maintenance of the unemployed, for if the lot of the unemployed was really desperate employers would have little difficulty in forcing those in work to accept wage cuts. The General Council had a further interest in the question of insurance. Instead of the various

[1] See Skidelsky, *Politicians and the Slump*.

separate forms of social provision – health insurance, unemployment insurance, old age pensions – they wished to create a
unified scheme of payments on a non-contributory basis. Part of
the idea behind this was to remove older men from the labour
market by enhanced pensions, thus creating more jobs for younger
workers now unemployed. At the other end of the age range the
T.U.C. wished to raise the school leaving age, thus taking the
youngest age groups off the labour market and again creating more
jobs. Bevin was the principal advocate of this scheme, and it had
formed an important part of the Mond–Turner Conference
Report on Unemployment, issued in March 1929. The Labour
Government had toyed briefly with the idea at the start of its
period of office, but nothing came of the matter.

The issue of Unemployment Insurance, however, was a live
one throughout the period of the Labour Government. The
Government, which was of course in a minority position, was
under constant pressure from the other parties to economise its
expenditure on unemployment benefit, and as the level of unemployment mounted the pressure became more insistent. In
October 1930 the Government announced the appointment of a
Royal Commission on Unemployment Insurance. This was
intended to delay the action demanded by the Opposition to curb
expenditure.[1] But the General Council did not see things in this
light, and felt that the Commission was merely intended to pave
the way for those reductions in benefit that the Opposition demanded. In January 1931 a deputation from the General Council led
by Citrine and Chairman Arthur Hayday met the Prime Minister
and Minister of Labour at Downing Street. A first-class row
ensued, in which Citrine accused the Government of setting up
the Royal Commission merely in order to produce the result
desired by the Opposition. Citrine also protested that there had
been no proper consultation with the T.U.C. as to the terms of
reference of the Commission. Although MacDonald assured the
Council that the Commission had only been set up because the
Liberals and Tories would not allow further Government borrow-
ing to finance unemployment benefit unless some gesture was
made, relations between the Government and the T.U.C. remained
strained. When the Royal Commission published its interim
report in June 1931 matters again came to a head. The majority

[1] Ibid. pp. 263–70.

report had recommended among other things increased worker contributions and reduced benefits. The General Council was adamant against this, and announced that massive demonstrations would be organised in the main industrial areas in opposition to the Report. The Government was in an unenviable position. Harried by its opponents to cut expenditure, any move in that direction brought it up against the militant opposition of its own supporters. In the end, MacDonald decided not to legislate on the basis of the Report's recommendations, but merely to deal with alleged abuses in the working of the system. Even here, however, the General Council was determined to allow him little room for manœuvre.

In June 1931 the Unemployment Insurance issue was still of relatively limited significance so far as the general economic position of Britain was concerned. During the next few weeks, however, the European financial crisis enveloped Britain, and there occurred a crisis of confidence in sterling. The threat to sterling was felt to stem less from the balance of payments deficit which the country was running than from the unbalanced budget of the Government, to which attention had been drawn by the publication of the May Committee's Report on 31 July. The Committee had been set up the previous March to make recommendations for cuts in Government expenditure. Like the Royal Commission on Unemployment Insurance before it, it was forced on the Government, which regarded it as a means of postponing action. But the Report of the Committee had the effect of publicising the budget deficit, and this helped to set off a crisis in confidence in sterling. Given this crisis the Labour Government was faced with a choice: it could devalue, or it could remove the cause of the crisis by drastically cutting expenditure and so bringing the budget into balance. Devaluation was not regarded as a possible alternative, and Ernest Bevin's advocacy of such a course in his addendum to the Macmillan Committee Report was highly unorthodox. However, the fact that Bevin and the General Council did see it as a possibility was bound to colour their reaction to attempts by the Government to restore a balanced budget.

The deepening economic crisis largely dominated the work of the General Council during 1931. In January the Economic Committee had decided to set on foot a thorough investigation into the economic problem, out of which it was hoped a definitive policy might emerge which could be presented to the Annual

Congress to be held in Bristol. Immediately, however, the pressing problem was the attack on wages that was being made in industry. In April one union wrote to the Council suggesting that a Conference of Executives might be convened 'to consider measures for meeting the attack on wages'. The suggestion was reminiscent of that made by George Hicks in 1922, when the movement was confronted with a similar situation. It was, however, noticeable that in 1931 nothing came of this suggestion, and one must assume that the Council definitely turned its back on any attempt to co-ordinate industrial action in resistance to wage cuts. Instead it merely reaffirmed publicly the viewpoint it had taken the year before in its evidence to the Macmillan Committee, stressing that wage-cutting could offer no solution for Britain's economic difficulties. But if the Council's influence on the industrial front was necessarily limited, it was destined to be decisive politically, through its influence upon the party which formed the Government of the day.

On 20 August the Cabinet Economy Committee appointed by MacDonald to find ways of balancing the budget, asked to see the General Council as a matter of urgency. At the meeting MacDonald made a vague opening statement about the need to close the gap between Government income and expenditure. After a protest by Citrine against these generalities Snowden, the Chancellor of the Exchequer, was more explicit. He said that the budget deficit could not be remedied by increased taxation alone, and that cuts in expenditure would be necessary. So far as the latter were concerned there were various possibilities. No direct cuts in unemployment benefit were proposed, although an increase in contributions and reduction in the duration of payments were suggested. Further proposals were cuts in the pay of public servants, such as teachers and police; reductions of grants made to local authorities to engage in relief works for the unemployed; and savings made through the Road Fund. The Council received these proposals as information and then retired to consider their position. This could hardly be in doubt in view of the stand they had taken in the past. At 9.30 in the evening the Council returned. They informed the Cabinet Sub-Committee that they could not agree to any of the proposals put before them. Any reduction in the standards of the unemployed was unthinkable. So far as cuts in the pay of public servants were concerned, Citrine suggested that this would merely intensify the pressure on wages in industry generally. It was difficult enough to resist wage cuts as things stood, if the proposals of the Government were carried out it would be impossible. Snowden commented that apparently the Council were opposed to all suggestions made for economies, to which Bevin and Citrine sardonically replied that the question of reducing Cabinet Ministers' salaries had not yet been touched on. The unbending T.U.C. line on Government expenditure was decisive in terminating the life of the second Labour Government, for after such a stand by the trade-union element in the party, MacDonald had little hope of carrying his Cabinet with him in a policy of drastic deflation. Thus on 24 August the Labour Administration was succeeded by a National Government, led by MacDonald, and composed of representatives of the three parties. The great bulk of Labour M.P.s, however, remained in opposition.

The role of the General Council during the 1931 financial crisis gave the lie to those who had held that by pursuing the path of co-operation with the employers, the Council was sacrificing the independence and integrity of the trade-union movement. Far from making the T.U.C. captives of the establishment, Mondism had proved to be an educational force, which resulted in the Council's taking a line in economic policy that was strikingly independent. It was the Labour Party leadership, whose vague and ill-defined socialism gave them no guide to policies to be pursued in the short run, who fell captives to the economic orthodoxy of the establishment. The General Council's policy during the financial crisis was independent of that of both the F.B.I. and the N.C.E.O., both of whom had come out in favour of cuts in public expenditure during the spring. In an exchange of letters between Citrine and Walker, the General Secretary of the F.B.I., during the height of the August crisis, it was agreed that the positions of the two sides were so far apart that no good purpose would be served by a joint meeting. On this issue, it was agreed to differ. There was therefore no question that contact with employers' organisations had undermined the T.U.C.'s independence. The performance of the second Labour Government indicated only too well that the real danger to the independence of the labour movement lay in continued reliance on emotive slogans as a substitute for constructive thought.

7 An Example to the Nation, 1931-9

I. THE 1930S – RESPONSIBILITY WITHOUT POWER

THE period between 1926 and 1931 had been one of reorientation for the T.U.C. Most of the radical proposals for internal change in the trade-union movement had been quietly dropped, so that increasingly their only advocates were found upon the extreme Left. Advocacy of massive co-ordinated industrial action and revolution became virtually synonymous, and the General Council set its face against both. Instead of proposing structural reform and a transfer of power to the centre, the General Council had sought to extend its influence in the movement by giving a more realistic definition of policy objectives, and in its handling of the economic problems of the day it certainly acquired a new sophistication and maturity. Undoubtedly the influence of Bevin and Citrine was decisive in this respect, although the part played by Arthur Pugh, and by Milne-Bailey as head of the Research Department, should not be overlooked.

This new approach could be of value to the movement in several ways. Internally, the T.U.C.'s grasp of the wide issues affecting the life of the workers might influence individual unions in their policies at industry level. For instance, the leadership's acceptance of the need for rationalisation, provided adequate safeguards existed for those made redundant, could influence the attitude of affiliated unions towards change in their own industries. The General Council could not, however, enforce a policy on this question. It could only make the unions aware of what was involved in any issue. Externally the T.U.C. could make its views known to both the national employers' organisations and the Government, in the hope their policies would conform as far as possible to its own views. Here again, however, there were severe limitations. The T.U.C. had not succeeded in establishing a National Industrial Council with the employers, so that the degree to which industry as a whole could agree upon common policy objectives was strictly limited. It was true that contact had been established with the F.B.I. and the N.C.E.O., but this proved to be no substitute for a permanent Council. The trouble was that the T.U.C. could make progress with the F.B.I., whose sphere of operation was general economic policy, but not with the N.C.E.O., which was concerned with purely labour matters. The consultations which the General Council had begun in 1930 with the F.B.I. on the question of a Commonwealth economic grouping, were continued through until 1932, and were felt to be of some use in the formulation of trade union policy on trading matters. Relations with the N.C.E.O., however, never got properly established. On the T.U.C.'s initiative talks were begun on the question of the displacement of labour due to rationalisation. The response of the Confederation was negative in the extreme, so that the talks tailed off without anything being achieved. The possibilities which the Mond–Turner talks had opened up, of the T.U.C. formulating general policy for industry as a whole on a joint basis with the employers' federations, thus never matured during the 1930s. The National Confederation was simply not willing to discuss general issues of vital concern to labour. This in turn reacted upon the General Council's internal influence, for the extent to which the Council could advocate new constructive policies upon affiliated unions was bound to be limited if employers insisted on restricting industrial relations to questions of wages and hours.

Given the unconstructive attitude of employers, the only other way in which the T.U.C. could make its policies count was by influencing the actions of the Government. The scope for this kind of activity was limited after 1931 by political considerations. The General Council had succeeded in preventing the Labour Government from embarking on a policy of drastic economies, but at a cost. For the Labour Government was replaced by a National Administration pledged to carry through these same economies. Furthermore, the National Government went to the polls in October 1931, and secured a devastating triumph, despite the fact that it had after all been forced to devalue. The Labour Party, minus a handful of its leaders who had joined the Coalition, fought the election in opposition to the Government. Its defeat was complete. The number of Labour M.P.s was reduced from 287 in 1929 to 52 after the 1931 election. Although the position was improved at the 1935 election, when 156 Labour M.P.s were elected, the Party was never within sight of forming a

Government throughout the decade of the 1930s. As during the 1924-9 period, therefore, the T.U.C. had to live with a Conservative Government, for this is what the National Government quickly became. The extent to which this Government was amenable to the T.U.C.'s point of view was obviously strictly limited, although it must be said that its approach to industrial relations was considerably more progressive than that of previous Conservative administrations.[1]

To a considerable degree therefore, the General Council of the 1930s was denied constructive outlets for its energies. The brilliance of its leadership, and the range and scope of its policies, stood in marked contrast to its actual power in the national community. Large-scale unemployment, which persisted throughout the decade, ensured that neither Government nor employers needed to pay too much attention to the trade union point of view. In this frustrating situation the Council devoted an increasing amount of time to activity within the Labour Party. It would be wrong to see in this any shift away from the course which Bevin and Citrine had set for the T.U.C. after 1926. Involvement in the Labour Party after 1931 may be seen as being in the nature of an investment by the General Council. Time and energy devoted to formulating political programmes for the future were necessary if the wasted opportunities of 1929-31 were not to be repeated. The weakness of the Parliamentary Labour Party after 1931 in fact gave the General Council the dominant voice in the Labour Movement, and it was determined to use its position to carry the political wing along what it regarded as the path of realism.[2]

2. PLANNING THE SOCIALIST FUTURE

The 1931 Congress at Bristol met in the interval between the collapse of the Labour Government and the General Election. The full implications of the August crisis were therefore not yet evident. Already, however, one feature that was to be characteristic of the 1930s stood clearly in evidence. This was the changed relationship of the T.U.C. to the Labour Party. From 1922 until

[1] See the chapter on Great Britain in H. A. Marquand and others, *Organised Labour in Four Continents* (1939) pp. 181-3.
[2] For the General Council's dominance of the Labour Party in the thirties see H. Pelling, *A Short History of the Labour Party*, (1962) ch. 5.

the final crisis in August 1931 the relationship of the industrial and political wings had been an uneasy one. Despite the loyalty of most trade unionists to MacDonald's leadership, the latter had never been on close terms with the union leaders. Nor, of course, had Snowden. Now, however, these two were outside the Party. The place of MacDonald as leader was taken by Arthur Henderson, the creator of the National Joint Council, and a long-standing advocate of close collaboration between the political and industrial wings. Henderson's presence at the Bristol Congress signified the new unity that prevailed. The two sides had in fact been working in close liaison ever since the formation of the National Administration, and on 27 August a joint meeting of the General Council, Labour Party Executive and Consultative Committee of the Parliamentary Labour Party had issued a manifesto proclaiming the basis of their opposition to the new Government. The proposed economy measures had been castigated as irrelevant to the solution of the country's economic difficulties. Indeed, in so far as they resulted in a reduction of mass purchasing power, they were merely calculated to aggravate the problem. The nature of the crisis, the manifesto argued, had been greatly exaggerated by financial interests who sought to reverse 'the social policy which in this country has within limits provided for the unemployed, the aged and the sick'. Unemployment benefit was a particular object of attack because it strengthened resistance to wage cuts. Arthur Hayday in his Presidential Address to the Congress elaborated these themes further, again pointing to the significance of Unemployment Insurance in maintaining wage levels. Hayday's speech reflected the united determination of the Labour Movement to resist the attack on its living standards, and although the election the following month was to prove a severe setback, the new unity of purpose of which he spoke was real enough. There was to be plenty of internal strife in the movement during the course of the 1930s, but the bond established between the political and industrial leadership was not to be broken. Six years later, at the 1937 Congress, Hugh Dalton the Chairman of the Labour Party declared: 'We on the political side are determined that this close co-operation shall continue up to and beyond our conquest of political power in this land'. The years 1945-51 were to demonstrate that this was not mere wishful thinking.

While much of the 1931 Congress was concerned with the crisis just passed, a good deal of the business concerned longer term economic developments. We saw in the last chapter how the Economic Committee had decided in the previous January to conduct a general investigation into the economic situation, with the object of framing a comprehensive policy for the industrial movement. The Committee reported to Congress that its work was not yet complete, but would be presented in its final form the following year. However, the lines on which the Committee were working was indicated in a Council resolution on Planning, which was moved by Arthur Pugh. The resolution welcomed 'the present tendency towards a planned and regulated economy in our national life'. It was hardly surprising that one delegate got up to say that in the present economic circumstances there seemed little to welcome. The Council had, however, shown itself to be remarkably sensitive to the trend of the times, for under the impact of world depression most governments were revising their attitudes, abandoning *laissez-faire* and moving tentatively towards greater intervention in the economy. The belief was gradually gaining ground that unrestricted competition bore part of the responsibility for depression, and that henceforward greater regulation of the economy would be needed. State intervention in the economy had numerous possible facets, but one in particular had attracted the General Council's attention so far as Britain was concerned. and this aspect of state intervention predated the world depression by some years. This was the creation by the Government of public corporations to manage or develop certain sectors of the economy. So far as transport was concerned, the Port of London Authority provided one example, dating from before 1914. In more recent years, however, the principle had been applied to electricity supply, broadcasting, and most recently of all, London transport. Even where industries were not actually taken over by public bodies, there were signs of Government preparedness to lay down certain regulations governing their functioning, as in case of the cartelisation of the coal industry in 1930, or the Road Traffic Act of the same year. This was to be a continuing trend during the thirties. The effect of all these measures was to restrict competition in their respective industries. This, as Citrine was to claim at Congress the following year, was in accord with the basic objectives of trade union policy. Restricted competition reduced the pressure on wage rates and so benefited workers in the industries concerned.

It was, however, recognised that mere cartelisation might benefit workers and employers in the industries concerned, but that these benefits would be exacted at the expense of the consumer, who would have to pay higher prices. This point was made in the Pugh resolution. The real objective of public regulation should be the more rational use of productive resources, thus raising productivity, and materially benefiting the community at large.

Congress accepted the resolution, but the general direction of the Council's economic policy was further revealed in two other items on the agenda of the Bristol Congress. One was a resolution on the iron and steel industry, again moved by Arthur Pugh, which involved the application of the above principles to this particular sector. The significant thing about this resolution was its advocacy of taking a major industry into public ownership, not on grounds of socialist ideology, but on straightforward economic grounds. Pugh wanted to bring iron and steel under 'the control of a public utility corporation, and to secure the mobilisation of the best organising ability, technical knowledge and experience for the effective organisation of the industry'. The fact that Pugh's proposals gave no emphasis to the question of securing workers' control, or active participation in management, resulted in a good deal of criticism, and his resolution passed narrowly. The question of workers' representation was raised explicitly in a resolution moved by J. Cliff of the T.G.W.U., calling upon the Government to accept the principle that when an industry was transferred to public ownership, the workers, through their trade-union representatives, should 'have an adequate and direct share in the control and administration of such industry or service'. Cliff had in mind the failure of the union to persuade the Minister of Transport of the need to appoint a labour representative on the London Passenger Transport Board. His resolution was carried, despite the reservations of some General Council members, and it became clear that an important issue had been raised. The socialisation of industry had long been advocated by Congress, but it was evident that divergent views existed as to what were the basic objectives to be attained through public ownership.

The 1931 Congress proved to be the starting point for a thorough debate on the long term objectives of T.U.C. policy, that was to continue throughout most of the decade. When the next year's Congress assembled at Newcastle the General Council placed before the delegates two major economic policy statements: one on fiscal policy, the other on public control and regulation of industry and trade. The report on fiscal policy drew attention to the shift that was taking place in capitalist economies away from unrestricted competition towards greater regulation of international trade. In February 1932 the National Government had definitely abandoned free trade and gone over to protection. The imposition of tariffs made possible a policy of discrimination in favour of the Commonwealth countries, and in July and August an Imperial Economic Conference met in Ottawa with the object of building up a system of imperial preference. The General Council had discussed these developments with the F.B.I., and the Government had invited the Council to nominate two Industrial Advisors to go to Ottawa along with the representatives of the employers, to advise on industrial questions. The Council agreed, and John Bromley, the year's Chairman, and Citrine duly attended the Conference. While the Council's report did not come down in favour of protection in principle, it felt that the new tariff arrangements should not be condemned automatically, before there was time to see how they worked. In general the Council favoured a flexible approach towards international trade, rather than a dogmatic Free Trade or Protectionist stand. Whether or not particular industries should be protected was a matter that ought to be decided with reference to the merits of each individual case, rather than upon the basis of an abstract principle. So far as Commonwealth economic co-operation was concerned, the Council had already come out in favour of this in 1930, but it did not regard this as a commitment to a specifically Protectionist policy. Finally, the Council was at pains to point out that in so far as greater Government regulation of international trade meant a movement away from *laissez-faire* and unrestrained competition, it was something which the trade union movement ought to welcome. It was a movement towards that planned development of the economy, in the interests of the whole community, that the Council leadership equated with Socialism.

There was some criticism of the Fiscal Report on the grounds that tariffs would reduce living standards, but Citrine pointed out that the Report did not advocate a Protectionist system, merely a flexible approach towards international trade, and Congress accepted his view by a large majority. The other major policy statement was a development of Pugh's Planning resolution of the previous year. The Report remarked on the tendency for public ownership or control of industry and trade to increase, and outlined the factors determining whether an industry or service should be placed under public control. So far as actual ownership was concerned, the Council favoured the public corporation method rather than direct operation by a Government department. Financially, it felt that these undertakings should stand on their own feet so far as possible, and should be free from Treasury control. In special cases subsidies could be provided by Parliament, but these were to be regarded as exceptional. The really thorny problem, so far as the labour movement was concerned, was the position of the workers in relation to the control of industry as a whole, and socialised industries in particular. So far as industry as a whole was concerned the General Council recommended the creation of an Industrial Council on the lines proposed by the Mond–Turner conferences in 1928. With regard to nationalised industries, the Report recommended that Boards of Management 'should consist of persons appointed by the Government solely on the ground of their fitness for the position, not excluding persons from any class but not selected as representing particular interests'. The latter, including the unions, were to be catered for by Advisory Committees set up by the industry. At the level of the individual plant, financial, commercial and technical matters were to be the responsibility of managers, appointed solely on the basis of competence to undertake the work. So far as labour questions were concerned – recruitment, dismissals, discipline, conditions – trade unions were to assume greater responsibility. Finally Works Councils were to be established on which the unions would represent the workers' side, and regular consultation was to take place on all internal matters not coming within the scope of the ordinary negotiating machinery. Here then was the Economic Committee's blueprint for the future organisation of industry, and on the basis of the principles laid down it proposed to draw up detailed plans for public ownership in a series of industries, beginning with iron and steel.

The Report aroused a good deal of controversy, for the preceding year Congress had accepted John Cliff's resolution to the effect that in nationalised industries workers should participate in management and control. Cliff now got up to attack the Council

for failing to embody this principle in its Report, and he moved its
reference back. The Report, he argued, gave labour merely
advisory functions. He wanted executive functions. Cramp, in
replying for the Council, argued that workers' representatives on
Boards of Management would be in an ambiguous position if they
were not in a majority. They would be associated with decisions
taken by the Board, even where these conflicted with the interests
of the workers. He implied that it would be better for unions to
retain independence of action, outside the managerial structure,
rather than become involved in a conflict of loyalties. The matter
was not finally resolved, however, the issue being left open for
consideration by the various unions.

The role of labour in the conduct of industry was an important
issue which the movement had to face. In 1932, however, the one
stark fact that overshadowed all other aspects of the economy
was massive unemployment. Unemployment had been bad in the
1920s, with a million continuously out of work, but the world
depression that had gathered momentum since 1929 made even
the twenties seem prosperous. 1932 was the darkest year of the
depression, when unemployment reached its peak. Of the insured
working population close to three million, or 22 per cent, were out
of work in 1932. While some improvement set in during 1933, the
level remained at over two million until 1936. Trade union membership, falling with the level of employment, reached its lowest
ebb in 1933, when there were fewer than four and a half million
members, compared with over eight million back in 1920. In some
ways, however, the T.U.C. remained strangely isolated from the
desolation that afflicted so many thousands in this era. At national
level it was true that the General Council had shown the greatest
concern over the level of unemployment, and in particular had
pressed upon the state its obligation to provide a decent maintenance for those out of work. The conflict with the Labour
Government in 1931 had largely centred upon this issue. But its
contact with the unemployed in the localities was limited. During
the early thirties numerous, and sometimes violent, demonstrations occurred, as the unemployed protested against the more
stringent administration of unemployment benefits, and against
the means test in particular. The General Council, was, however,
reluctant to associate itself with such militancy, just as during the
General Strike it had been anxious not to allow local militants to

get out of control. The problem was of course Communism, for the principal organisation mobilising the unemployed in demonstrations and hunger marches was the National Unemployed Workers' Committee Movement, a Communist front organisation. It will be remembered that the Council had severed its relationship with this body in 1927. At the 1932 Congress a deputation of unemployed workers was refused admittance to Congress, on the grounds of their association with the Committee Movement. The Council did, however, recognise a responsibility towards the organisation of the unemployed. Back in 1927 it had attempted to establish Unemployed Associations, but the initiative had not been favourably received by affiliated unions. Towards the end of 1931 the attempt had been renewed. In making its report to the 1932 Congress the Council stressed that it had been forced to reconsider the position owing to the fact that other bodies were moving into the field – political parties, religious bodies, philanthropic institutions, and local trade unionists acting in an unofficial capacity. It had therefore recommended the local Trades Councils to set up Associations, and by the time of the Newcastle Congress fifty-eight were in existence. In the event, however, the Associations did not prove a success. Their activities were narrowly defined, and the anxiety to keep them under control was evident from the beginning. There was a reluctance to provide facilities for the unemployed to engage in constructive employment, for fear of creating competition which would affect those in work. Too much emphasis was laid upon using the Associations as a source of future union recruitment, by exacting a pledge from members that they would join a union when they found work. Finally, so far as militant action was concerned, they could not compete with the Communist-inspired movement. It is difficult to escape the conclusion that the reasons for their formation were essentially negative, reflecting the narrow self-interest of individual unions, and the ideological antagonism of the T.U.C. leadership to Communist militancy.

When the T.U.C. met at Brighton in 1933 attention was largely focused on developments abroad, for in Germany and in the U.S.A. the world depression had resulted in major political upheavals that were full of significance for Britain. In the U.S.A. the 1932 Presidential election had resulted in the triumph of Roosevelt and the Democratic Party. A programme of national recovery was launched immediately; the New Deal era had begun. The developments in America made a profound impression on trade-union leaders in Britain. At the Brighton Congress delegates listened to a speech given by a fraternal delegate from the American Federation of Labour on the subject of the new recovery legislation. President Walkden devoted a large part of his opening address to the matter, and the General Council put down a special resolution on recovery policy that was moved by Citrine. The attraction of Roosevelt's policy to T.U.C. leaders was simply that it was their own policy also, only in this case it was actually being implemented by the Government of a major industrial nation. The extent to which New Deal policies were anticipated in the trade-union movement is well illustrated by the General Council's international activities. Since the end of the 1920s the International Federation of Trades Unions had been devoting much thought to economic policy, paralleling developments in the T.U.C. The latter's role in the Federation was an extremely active one, and in 1928 Citrine became its President. In 1931 a joint committee of the Federation and the Labour and Socialist International investigated the unemployment problem, and produced a series of resolutions. Most of these corresponded closely with T.U.C. policy, as for instance on the need to resist a reduction in purchasing power through wage cuts, and on the need for adequate maintenance of the unemployed. Particularly interesting, however, was the resolution on public works:

In contradiction to the capitalist view which demands a reduction of state expenditure in times of economic crisis, only the greatest possible increase in public expenditure for productive work in times of crisis can lessen the disproportion between the efficiency of the productive forces of the nation and the consumption which falls short of this.

In its emphasis on public expenditure, and on the maintenance of wage levels, the American recovery programme corresponded exactly with that recommended by the union movement.

The General Council's resolution on industrial recovery at the 1933 Congress called upon the National Government to follow the American example. It called upon the Government to initiate schemes of public works, to enact a maximum working week of forty hours without reduction of wages, to prohibit child labour under sixteen years of age and to raise the school-leaving age to sixteen, to raise wages in the public services, to make more liberal provision for pensioning aged workers, 'and generally to take all possible measures for increasing the purchasing power of the masses'. The General Council was, however, careful to stress that it regarded this as essentially an emergency programme which in no way altered its commitment to public ownership and economic planning as the long-term goals of the movement. When the resolution was debated one or two speakers reiterated this point, but the resolution passed with but one opponent.

3. FACING UP TO FASCISM – THE OPENING PHASE

The other major international event since the Newcastle gathering was of a quite different order, yet, like the New Deal, it also had its roots in mass unemployment. In Germany, however, the reaction to economic misery had taken the form of political extremism, with the result that the Nazi Party under Hitler's leadership had taken control in Berlin. From 1933 until the outbreak of war the menace of Fascism was to have a prominent place on the agenda of Annual Congress. Probably more than any other institution in Britain the T.U.C. showed its concern at the rise of Fascism abroad. This was no accident, for the General Council was almost uniquely well placed to observe the workings of these odious regimes. Trade unions were almost the first institutions to be smashed by the Fascists upon their assumption of power, and the T.U.C. through its membership of the I.F.T.U. was only too well informed as to what was the fate of the unions in Germany and elsewhere. The approach of the General Council towards Fascism, however, came to differ markedly from that of other elements in the labour movement, particularly the politicians on the left of the Labour Party. The viewpoint to which the Council was to adhere throughout the thirties was set forth at the 1933 Congress in a crucial policy statement, entitled 'Dictatorship and the Trade Union Movement'. The statement described the conditions which had given rise to the Nazi Movement in Germany, including the atmosphere of violence and political extremism of both Right and Left. At this period the Fascist menace was seen rather as an internal than as an external threat, and the Report considered the possible dangers of a Fascist take-over in Britain. This was considered unlikely in so far as the British situation differed markedly from the German, although a common element was provided by the high level of unemployment. The main point the Report was anxious to stress was that the trade unions would be making a disastrous mistake if they allowed the menace of Fascism to beguile them into an alliance with the Communists. Alliance with Communism would only drag the country into the same climate of violence and anarchy which had permitted the Nazis to take power in Germany. For force on the Left would be met with force on the Right. As Citrine said in moving the acceptance of the Report – 'every time they made a Communist they made a Fascist'. Beyond this the Report challenged the assumption that the union movement had in any case anything in common with Communism. It became a commonplace in left-wing circles during the thirties to regard political development in terms of a straightforward confrontation between the forces of the Left and those of the Right. In this analysis the National Government in Britain was regarded as little better than a Fascist regime. The 1933 T.U.C. Report took a different view. Whatever might be thought of the existing Government, freedom in Britain was a reality. Trade unions enjoyed rights in Britain which they held neither in Fascist nor in Communist countries. The real confrontation was between the forces of democracy and those of dictatorship, whether of the Right or of the Left. The full importance of this T.U.C. viewpoint only became apparent later, when the menace of Fascism came to be seen as an external rather than an internal threat. For at this juncture the question arose in labour circles as to whether the movement would be justified in supporting a British rearmament programme while a Tory Government was in power. The Left wing of the Labour Party was loath to give such support, but the General Council's higher valuation of the democratic system impelled it to argue in favour of equipping the Government with the means to meet the totalitarian challenge from outside. The immediate significance of the Report was its rejection of any united front with the Communists in Britain. Already in 1933 the General Council and the Labour Party had received communications from the Communist Party inviting them to send representatives to a Conference 'with a view to forming a united front of working class organisations against Fascism'. The Council reported to Congress that it had refused the invitation.

The General Council's Report came in for plenty of criticism from Communists and their sympathisers at Congress, and Aneurin Bevan, as a delegate of the Miners, seconded its reference back. Citrine's mastery of the situation was, however, complete and his policy triumphed by an overwhelming majority. The Report itself, and the manner in which it had been presented to Congress, reflected the high quality of his leadership. Citrine was in action again when the issue of worker representation in nationalised industries reappeared. After the criticisms of the General Council's line at Newcastle consultations had taken place with the Labour Party, and the Council now reported that it accepted the right of the unions to nominate persons for appointment to Boards of Management. There the matter rested for the moment. However, neither then, nor later, did it change its view that unionists serving on such Boards ought *not* to act in a representative capacity, thereby ruling out any element of workers' control.

In 1834 a group of Dorsetshire agricultural labourers had been sentenced to transportation for trade union activities; they became known as the Tolpuddle Martyrs. 1934 was the centenary of their 'martyrdom' and Congress that year was held at Weymouth, in order to be near Tolpuddle, where tribute was to be paid to their memory. It was an appropriate moment to remember sacrifices made on behalf of the labour movement for on the Continent the forces of reaction were engaged in savage repression of independent labour organisation. In 1933 it had been Germany, in 1934 it was Austria, where the Dollfuss regime had gunned down socialists and unionists in the streets of Vienna. The Austrian capital, under a socialist municipal government, had been a show-piece of the Continental labour movement. British unionists had visited it, and had admired the fine modern apartment buildings erected for the workers of the city. Now all this was a thing of the past. The delegates at Weymouth rose, and stood in silence, in honour of Austrian workers who had been killed.

The preoccupations of this Congress were essentially the same as those of the previous year, but A. Conley in his Presidential speech struck one note that had not been heard since 1926. The magic word co-ordination was conjured up once more, and Conley asked the delegates:

Is it not wise and timely to consider the simultaneous presentation to employers in all industries of a carefully planned programme of wage increases . . .which each union or group of unions, with the assistance or guidance of the General Council, can make a matter of negotiation in the trades with which they are concerned.

Now that the depression had done its worst, and economic activity was very slowly on the upturn, Conley's remarks were perhaps timely in a tactical sense. They were also timely in the sense that sufficient time had now elapsed since the debacle of 1926 for it to be possible to resume rational consideration of the Council's role in industry. In the event, however, the focus of the T.U.C.'s activities remained unaltered during the thirties. They continued to revolve around general policy issues, following the course that had been set by the leadership at the end of the twenties.

The 1934 Congress saw the appearance of the first of the Council's Reports on the nationalisation of specific industries. The Report on the Socialisation of Iron and Steel followed in all essentials the lines laid down by the Council in 1932, including the tacit rejection of the doctrine of workers' control. Appointments to the Central Board were to be on grounds of competence and appointees holding offices in trade unions were to relinquish them on taking up their new duties. In one respect the Report, like Conley's speech, called up echoes of the early twenties, for it stressed that public ownership of the steel industry would require structural reform of the unions. 'An obvious step in that direction', the Report said, 'must be the complete unification of trade union organisation, which must conform to that of the industry.' Industrial unionism was not dead, merely sleeping. The following year the Council produced a scheme for the cotton industry, which followed almost exactly the iron and steel scheme, and included the recommendation that trade-union structure conform to that of the industry. A further similar report on coal was presented in 1936. Since these were long-term policy documents, dependent for their implementation upon the advent of a Labour Government, the structural issue was somewhat academic. However, their conclusion so far as trade-union organisation was concerned represented a departure from the 1927 Report on structure, with its rejection of a planned industrial union structure. The contradiction did not arouse comment.

The truth was that T.U.C. leaders were increasingly absorbed in international questions, and ideological issues that arose out of them. Whereas between 1927 and 1932 General Council activity was concentrated upon economic problems, after 1933 interest centred increasingly upon developments on the Continent. With this went another change. Between 1921 and 1931 the respective spheres of activity of the industrial and political wings of the movement had been fairly clearly defined, and their leaderships distinct. After 1931 this ceased to be the case. The Parliamentary weakness of the Labour Party made it essentially dependent upon the trade-union movement, and increasingly the tendency was for the T.U.C. leaders to be drawn into general policy formation for the whole movement. Symptomatic of this new state of affairs was the role of the National Joint Council, on which the General Council held half the seats. This came to function as a 'Cabinet of Labour', as Arthur Henderson had originally planned, and it laid down policy on the whole range of issues which affected the movement. Its decisions were referred first to the Annual Congress held in September, and then to the Labour Party Conference that followed in October. In this way the two sides of the movement tended to function in the thirties as a single entity. In 1935 the National Joint Council was renamed the National Council of Labour, which was a title more in keeping with its supreme position. On the Council the real influence belonged to the T.U.C. leaders, Bevin and Citrine in particular. This influence they used in the main to alert the movement to the menace of totalitarianism, whether of the Right or of the Left.

At the Weymouth Congress the General Council reported that through the National Joint Council the movement had rejected further attempts by the Communist Party to mobilise a United Front. It also reported that the Joint Council had declared its policy on the issue of prevention of war through strike action. This was a favourite theme of the Left, and the Joint Council's approach to the problem bore all the hallmarks of Bevin's and Citrine's realism. The Report pointed out that reliance on industrial action by the workers to stop a war was a dangerous delusion. It had not of course worked in 1914, but quite apart from that there was the likelihood that in the context of the 1930s aggressive action would come from countries where the labour movement was weak or non-existent, such as Germany, Italy and Japan. Industrial action in these countries was impossible, and so therefore was the whole policy of strikes to prevent war. The General Council offered its own contribution to the question of war prevention in a Report to the 1934 Congress, entitled 'Peace and War'. Basically, their approach was to rely upon a system of collective security operated through the League of Nations. They recognised, however, that such a system of collective security might entail the use of armed force to restrain aggressor nations. When the Report was debated the Left attacked the idea that any war fought by capitalist governments could be justified. As one speaker said, 'There are no aggressive nations. Only aggressive capitalists'. Citrine, in reply, retorted that the argument that it was impossible to organise collective security while capitalism prevailed simply meant wringing one's hands and waiting for war to come along. The pro-Communist group were a tiny minority at Congress, and the Council's view prevailed.

When Congress met the following year at Margate the issue of collective security through the League of Nations dominated all other considerations, for the Abyssinian crisis was at its height and as President Kean pointed out to the delegates, the reputation of the League would stand or fall according to whether or not it was successful in coercing Italy into keeping the peace. If the League failed in this crisis, it would be clear that collective security was doomed. While the international crisis was foremost in the minds of delegates the continued revival of the economy at home resulted in some consideration of industrial issues. Conley's suggestion of the year before, that the General Council should co-ordinate a forward movement for wage increases, aroused some interest, although in the end nothing came of it. The other issue which sprang out of the limited economic revival was the question of expanding union membership. Trade-union membership had reached its lowest ebb in the inter-war period in 1933. When the 1935 Congress met, however, membership was on the increase, if only slowly. The problem of membership expansion was that many of the traditional bastions of union strength were in declining industries, such as coal and cotton, so that future growth would depend on enrolling workers in the more modern mass production industries, such as automobiles, and in the expanding service sector of the economy, embracing such occupations as retail distribution, insurance and banking. The work of organising recruitment campaigns devolved upon the Trades Councils, and by 1935 the General Council had come to regard them as the recruiting agencies for the movement. The Trades Councils organised a number of membership drives in the centres of the newer industries, such as Slough and Birmingham, but inter-union rivalries tended to limit their effectiveness, as in the case of the 'Back to the Unions' campaign of 1923. It must be said that drive from the centre was notably lacking in the thirties when it came to membership expansion, and that the results achieved were correspondingly limited. Distrust of unofficial activity at local level continued to inhibit the T.U.C.'s effectiveness as an industrial body, and it was noticeable that more time was taken up at the Congresses of 1935 and 1936 in the proscription of the Communists than was devoted to organising matters. The Council had issued during the course of 1935 circulars 16 and 17, the former aimed at the Trades Councils, the latter at affiliated unions. The circular to the Councils was to the effect that T.U.C. recognition would be withdrawn in cases where Councils accepted delegates from either Communist or Fascist organisations. The other circular asked affiliated unions to amend their rules so as to disqualify 'members of disruptive bodies from holding office'. Forty-one unions agreed to this policy, twenty-five refused, and many others remained indifferent. At the Margate Conference there was considerable hostility shown to the Council's policy, especially towards Circular 17, and the reference back was defeated by only a narrow majority.

4. FACING UP TO FASCISM – THE FINAL PHASE

After 1935 T.U.C. leadership on international matters passed into its final and most significant phase. The change corresponded with a shift in the policy of the National Government towards rearmament. Aware from the beginning of the possibility of Fascist aggression, Citrine and Bevin had been up against the problem that such a menace could only be countered by force. The movement, however, contained a large pacifist element; indeed the Parliamentary Labour Party leader during the first half of the decade, George Lansbury, was a pacifist.[1] Furthermore, as we have seen, among left-wing elements the view prevailed that all capitalist governments were potentially aggressive and that

---

[1] Lansbury took over the leadership from Henderson in 1932. Henderson, though not a pacifist, was himself an ardent champion of disarmament, and in fact acted as President of the Disarmament Conference at Geneva in the early thirties.

therefore no constructive measures could be taken to preserve the peace while capitalism survived. In face of this kind of opposition the General Council had tried at the Weymouth and Margate Congresses to get the unions to accept the idea of using force to resist the Dictators, through the machinery of the League of Nations. Armaments would not therefore have the stigma of militarism, because they would be used by a kind of international police force. This policy the movement, as we have seen, was prepared to accept. However, after the Margate Congress came Mussolini's successful conquest of Abyssinia, which, as had been forecast, went far to discredit the idea of collective security through the League. A further blow followed in 1936, when Hitler marched into the demilitarised Rhineland. The effect of these developments was to force the Council's leadership into a realisation that, in the short run at any rate, the League was likely to prove ineffective in resisting the Dictators. That being so, the only way in which they could be resisted was by individual nations, including Britain, equipping themselves with armaments. It was realised that this would be unpalatable to the movement, but it was a fact that had to be faced.

When the 1936 Congress met at Plymouth the National Council of Labour had not yet worked out a revised policy to put before the movement. Bevin, however, stressed that such a revision would be necessary, and he warned:

If in certain aspects it means uprooting some of our cherished ideals and facing the issue fairly in the light of the development of Fascism, we must do it for the Movement and for the sake of posterity.

The immediate issue facing the movement, however, was the Spanish Civil War, which had broken out earlier in 1936. The National Council had here come out in favour of non-intervention, largely as a result of the French Government's support for the policy, this Government being socialist in composition. The policy came in for much criticism at Congress and was abandoned by the Council of Labour shortly afterwards, when it became clear that the policy was totally ineffective in preventing German and Italian intervention on the side of Franco's rebels. The Spanish War in which a United or Popular Front Government confronted the combined forces of the Right, reinforced the tendency in the movement to see world politics in terms of a confrontation between Left and Right, rather than between Democracy and Totalitarianism. The General Council, however, retained its hostility to any Popular Front movement in Britain, and a National Council of Labour statement to this effect was inserted in the Council's annual report. In view of the bitter disillusionment that the Spanish conflict was to bring to those idealists who had believed in cooperation with Communism, the standpoint taken by the Council may be said to have been vindicated by subsequent events. So far as domestic issues were concerned, the 1936 Congress was unremarkable. A flippant speech by Bevin succeeded in securing the rejection of a proposal that an enquiry should be carried out into trade-union structure with the objective of bringing it into line with the requirements of modern industry. All that needs to be said about this episode was that the proposal was made by an industrial union (N.U.R.), and opposed principally by spokesmen from a general union (T.G.W.U.) and a craft union (A.S.L.E.F.)! On a personal note, the General Council reported the death of W. Milne-Bailey, who had played such a large part in the development of the T.U.C.'s economic policy. His successor at the Research Department was George Woodcock.

In the interval between the Plymouth Congress of 1936 and that at Norwich in 1937 the National Council of Labour carried out its revision of T.U.C. international policy. It was fortunate that the chairman of the Labour Party Executive that year was Hugh Dalton, whose views on foreign policy were in close accord with those of Citrine and Bevin. By a further happy coincidence Bevin was chairman of the General Council that year. As Bevin's biographer has pointed out,[1] this must have seemed at the time to have been the climax of his career, for his mind was already turning to retirement. His address as President at Norwich, where he spoke of his pride in being Congress President and of his deep attachment to the union movement, reads almost like a farewell, and is indeed moving. It was, however, Citrine who dominated the business proceedings of Congress. The revised policy statement drawn up by the National Council of Labour was in some respects an ambiguous document. It argued from the basis that collective security through the League of Nations had clearly broken down, but the logical deduction from this, that Britain must be equipped

[1] Bullock, *The Life and Times of Ernest Bevin, 1881-1940*, vol. 1, pp. 614-16.

with armaments to resist the Dictators, was couched in a somewhat confusing form, for it seemed to be arguing only in favour of equipping a Labour Government of Britain with arms, and not the existing Government. Citrine in introducing the Report gave an extremely lucid analysis of the development of T.U.C. policy, but he could not disguise the ambiguity of the Report that had finally emerged. When the debate began Arthur Horner and Aneurin Bevan of the Miners focused attention on this ambiguity. They wanted a clear statement as to whether or not the General Council was suggesting that the arms programme of the existing National Government ought to be supported. If the Council was arguing for support, Bevan was opposed. He argued that the Government was not opposing Fascism, which the Report admitted, 'therefore you don't get opposition to the Fascist powers by voting for the Government's arms programme.' Citrine's reply constituted probably the finest speech he ever made to Congress, and it more than compensated for the ambiguity of the Report. He argued that rearmament had to be supported *now*, because the next election was not until 1940, when, assuming Labour was then returned to power, it would probably be too late to start rearming. He dismissed as ridiculous the argument that the National Government could not be trusted with armaments:

I frankly ask those who put that argument, do they really believe that any British Government would dare to pledge the forces of this country behind the Fascist powers?

If the Labour movement counted for anything, argued Citrine, such an attempt would involve the Government in civil war. It was not a question of supporting Government policy, merely of ensuring that Britain was adequately defended. Labour could not press the Government to stand up to the Dictators and at the same time oppose the manufacture of arms which alone made a firmer stand possible. The reference back was defeated by 3,544,000 votes to 224,000. The policy was confirmed at the Labour Party Conference at Bournemouth with the help of Bevin's forceful advocacy. The labour movement now accepted the full implications of its policy of resistance to Fascism.

5. ACHIEVEMENT – WITHIN LIMITS

The creation of a realistic and viable foreign policy for the labour movement was the greatest achievement of the General Council in the 1930s, and the achievement was in all essentials the work of Citrine and Bevin. It was of a piece with their efforts in the economic sphere in the period prior to 1933. Out of a welter of slogans, muddle and emotion they had carved a rational policy. As in economic, so in foreign policy, however, the Council was powerless to alter the drift of Government policy. Its recovery programme of 1933 had gone unheeded, its call for resistance to the Dictators was ignored also. The Government of Britain was in the hands of men of lesser stature than Bevin and Citrine, who were forced to watch on the sidelines as the forces of darkness gathered strength across the Channel.

The Government did, however, rearm, even if it continued its policy of appeasing the Fascists. In March 1938 Chamberlain invited the General Council to 10 Downing Street in order to ask for its goodwill and help in an acceleration of the armament programme. It was, incidentally, the first official visit of the Council to No. 10 since the General Strike. The talks in March, and a further meeting in May, were not very satisfactory as the Government had nothing specific to place before the T.U.C. Furthermore, Congress was of course fundamentally opposed to the Government's policy of appeasement. However, the General Council justified its meetings with Chamberlain on the grounds that it was an industrial body, and that it had therefore a responsibility to meet the Government on any issue likely to affect general condition in industry, irrespective of the politics of that Government. In any case, having decided at Norwich to support the rearmament programme, the T.U.C. could not absolve itself from responsibility in supporting the carrying out of that programme. There was, however, a good deal of criticism of the General Council at the Blackpool Congress of 1938, particularly from the Amalgamated Engineering Union, the union chiefly involved in the munitions industry. While Congress supported the Council's policy by an overwhelming majority, the issue clearly raised the limitations of the T.U.C.'s influence when it came to straightforward industrial activity. So long as its sphere of activity was on the general policy level its authority in the movement was great, but the brush with the A.E.U. indicated that affiliated unions were as jealous as ever of their autonomy, when it came to translating general policy into concrete industrial practice affecting the spheres of action of affiliated unions.

This was the great disappointment of the inter-war period so far as the General Council's history was concerned. When Citrine had entered the service of Congress in 1924 he had shared the hopes of Fred Bramley that the T.U.C. would become, as the 1924 General Council report expressed it, 'not merely an effective expression of industrial activity, but an efficient executive instrument to translate those expressions into practical realisation.' It had not come within sight of this objective, and in defending the Council against the criticisms of the A.E.U. at the 1938 Congress Citrine faced up to this unpalatable fact:

The unions have been committed to nothing for the simple reason, apart from any other consideration, that the Council have no powers to commit any union to anything.... On the other hand the General Council has some responsibility for general policy. The General Council was set up with the object of ultimately forming something like a general staff for labour, and the first function of a central body, even if it has not got those powers, is surely to do something to try and co-ordinate policy, to try to co-ordinate the action of its unions.

This, however, was the lament of a full-time T.U.C. officer, and it is doubtful whether the ordinary members of Council, as officers of individual unions as well as T.U.C. leaders, much regretted the lack of central executive power. Since 1926 they had certainly not exerted themselves to obtain it.

The next year's Congress at Bridlington, held at the moment when Britain at last 'stood up' to the Dictators, and declared war on Germany, highlighted the second major disappointment of the inter-war period, so far as T.U.C. influence was concerned. This was the failure to achieve any radical reform of union structure. The General Council's report for 1939 contained proposals for the development of the principles dealing with inter-union disputes, first laid down at Hull in 1924. It drew attention to the competitive nature of inter-union relationships which 'did not reflect credit on trade unionism'. Yet so long as no attempt was made at a more rational definition of union jurisdiction, so long would the unsatisfactory position continue. Neither the Hull nor the Bridlington rules could do more than contain the degree of inter-union friction, for they dealt with the symptoms, not the disease. Although the General Council had come down against a rational scheme of structural reform in 1927, it did so not because such a scheme was undesirable, but because no consensus existed on which to base reorganisation. This absence of consensus had been well illustrated as recently as 1936, as we saw above. The danger was that inaction on this question would sap the vitality of the movement in the long run.

Granted the limitations of the General Council's influence, it was none the less true that tremendous development had taken place in its authority since its creation in 1921. There was no area of policy of general concern to labour with which it did not concern itself. Leaving aside the major issues which have been the concern of this and earlier chapters, the Council dealt with Workmen's Compensation, Holidays with Pay, the Forty-Hour Week, the Depressed Areas, Education, Trade Boards, and scores of other questions. It set up advisory committees with unions in particular industries, and with outside bodies, including even scientists, medical practitioners, and experts on colonial development. It was active in the International Labour Organisation and the International Federation of Trade Unions. It controlled the *Daily Herald*, with a daily circulation of two million in the late thirties. It was asked to give evidence to, and nominate representatives to serve on, numerous committees and inquiries. Its leaders were national figures. Citrine and Pugh were knighted in the mid-thirties. The enhanced standing of the Council, both within the movement and outside it, had been achieved at a time not of overall trade-union strength, but of weakness, for total membership was still not back to the level of 1920 when World War II broke out. Furthermore it had occurred despite the most disastrous setback to the movement in the twentieth century, the 1926 General Strike, a setback be it noted in which the General Council was directly implicated. That its authority should have been enhanced despite these things reflected the outstanding calibre of its leadership. If there is one striking feature of T.U.C. history during the 1926-39 period it is the role of T.U.C. General Secretary, Walter Citrine. Annual Congress came almost to revolve around his lucid policy statements. Without him and Bevin there would surely have been a different story to tell in the post-1926 era.

8 The Fourth Estate, 1939-57

1. THE WAR EFFORT — A TURNING POINT FOR LABOUR

THE voice of the T.U.C. in the 1930s had been a voice in the wilderness. Neither on the issue of unemployment, nor on that of resistance to the Dictators, had the Government heeded its advice. The occupation of Prague by Hitler, in March 1939, at last altered Government policy so far as the external threat was concerned. Belatedly a stand was made against further Fascist aggression, and preparations were speeded up in readiness for the war that now seemed inevitable. The frustrations of the T.U.C. leadership were not at an end, however, for while they had supported resistance and rearmament, they expected that when the Government finally moved to put the nation on a warlike footing it would do so in consultation with them. Given its commitment to resist Fascism the Council was anxious to assist in such preparations, and at a special conference of executives held in London in May 1939 it presented detailed proposals for the organisation of labour in wartime, including the active participation of the unions in the solution of the problems of labour supply. It also proposed the setting up of a tripartite National Advisory Council to the Ministry of Labour, composed of unionists, employers, and civil servants. This initiative by the labour movement was ignored by the Chamberlain Government. Months passed, and at last the war came. In October the Minister of Labour did in fact set up the Advisory Council suggested, but a Ministry of Supply had been created without any consultation with the unions or provision for their representation on its committees. Exasperated, the General Council interviewed Chamberlain on 5 October. Citrine told the Prime Minister that the unions wanted participation in the work of all Government departments where working-class matters were considered. This was the price of their active support of the war effort. The meeting proved to be a turning point. Chamberlain accepted the T.U.C.'s viewpoint, and a directive was issued to all Government departments emphasising the need for complete co-operation with the trade unions.

The truth was that the coming of war had transformed the bargaining power of labour, and that sooner or later the Government would have to recognise this fact. The point was well put by Ernest Bevin:

It must be appreciated that in their heart of hearts the powers that be are anti-trade union . . . The Ministers and Departments have treated Labour with absolute contempt. Yet without the great trade union movement the Forces cannot be supplied with munitions nor the country with food . . . We do not desire to be invited to serve on any committee or body as an act of patronage. We represent probably the most vital factor in the state: without our people this war cannot be won nor the life of the country be carried on.

Before 1939 labour had been in only too plentiful supply. Total conflict changed all this. Manpower became the scarcest and most vital of the nation's resources. The wastage of this resource, which had occurred in the thirties, was no longer conceivable. As the war progressed it was manpower, not finance, that set the final limit to the national effort. The manpower budget superseded the financial budget in the control of the economy. The status of labour, and therefore of the trade unions, was transformed.

Belatedly, as we have seen, the Chamberlain Government recognised the logic of the new situation, and the full co-operation of the unions in the mobilisation of labour was enlisted. But the basis of co-operation remained an uneasy one, for the will of the Government to effectively organise national resistance was bound to remain suspect. Their record of appeasing the Dictators during the thirties counted heavily against them. It was, therefore, the formation of the Churchill Coalition in May 1940 which really signified a break with the past, and the possibility of a united national effort. Especially significant from the standpoint of the T.U.C. was Churchill's choice of a new Minister of Labour for his Government. The post went to Ernest Bevin. The qualities which Bevin had shown as General Secretary of the T.G.W.U., and as a member of the General Council, were now transferred to securing the most effective use of manpower in the national interest.

The first thing that was noticeable about Bevin's handling of his gigantic task was that he adhered, as far as was possible in the circumstances, to the principle of 'voluntarism' characteristic of

British industrial relations.[1] Parliament quickly armed him with a vast battery of powers to regulate the labour market by the issuing of orders, as for instance to transfer people between jobs and areas or to secure dilution of skilled work. Bevin, however, regarded compulsion as a weapon of last resort, and sought to achieve the necessary adjustments to a wartime economy so far as possible by enlisting the voluntary co-operation of unions and employers' organisations. In so far as it was necessary to issue orders, his method was to try to formulate these orders on the basis of a policy agreed in advance with the organisations in industry. In this he was following a fundamental axiom of T.U.C. policy, which in face of the continual growth of state power had shown itself anxious to preserve the independence of the unions. During the Mond–Turner Conferences it had declared itself in favour of a system of industrial self-government through a National Industrial Council. Bevin accepted the principle of voluntary self-government in industry, it was indeed part of that wider freedom which they were fighting to defend, but he gave it a tripartite basis, the Government functioning along with the representatives of the two sides of industry.

Bevin's appointment as Minister of Labour thus meant active trade union participation in the war effort. This was shown from the beginning, and during the first week when he was preparing proposals for submission to the Cabinet he kept in close touch with Citrine as T.U.C. General Secretary. Furthermore, on 25 May 1940, he set out his plans to a conference of trade union executives. A quite new relationship between the state and the trade unions had been established. The General Council already had some formal consultative machinery with the Ministry of Labour at the time Bevin was appointed. This took the form of the National Advisory Council, whose creation the T.U.C. had recommended back in the spring of 1939. Bevin's predecessor at the Ministry had, however, made little use of this machinery. Bevin now suggested to the two sides of industry that the Council was too large to function effectively as an instrument of practical co-operation, and he therefore replaced it by a Joint Consultative Committee. This body was composed of seven representatives from the Employers' Confederation and seven from the T.U.C.

[1] For Bevin's role at the Ministry of Labour see A. Bullock, *The Life and Times of Ernest Bevin, 1940–1945* (1967) vol. 2.

and was chaired by the Minister. That Bevin meant what he said about co-operation was made clear when he invited the Committee to consider the most immediate problem with which he was confronted, namely, how to cope with the problem of wage claims and strikes in wartime. As in the First World War, it was clear that interruptions to production through industrial disputes could not be tolerated, and a way had to be found of obviating them. The proposal which the Committee came up with was that existing wage negotiating machinery should be retained in existence, but that where a settlement could not be reached voluntarily, it should be referred to arbitration, and the award then made ought to be binding. Strikes and lock-outs were to be prohibited. This solution appealed to Bevin as retaining as far as possible existing voluntary negotiating machinery, merely substituting compulsory arbitration for industrial action. The policy thus agreed by the Committee was enforced through Order No. 1305. The practice that had been initiated, of real consultation with industry on orders to be issued, was continued, and through its representation on the Joint Consultative Committee the General Council was enabled to exert a real influence on labour policy.

The policy of continued reliance upon normal collective bargaining machinery in wartime had its critics in the Government and outside, and Bevin was under considerable pressure to revise it. Criticism rested on the grounds that if negotiating freedom was retained this would lead to excessive wage increases resulting in inflation.[1] The Treasury in particular was in favour of direct Government control of wages. Bevin knew that such a policy would be unacceptable to the unions; nevertheless he agreed to meet the General Council, along with the Chancellor of the Exchequer, in order to draw attention to the need for restraint in making wage claims. The meeting took place in July 1941, and Citrine affirmed the opposition of the T.U.C. to control of wages. This was again made clear at the 1941 Congress. In the event, Bevin was able to prevail over his opponents in the Government, and the T.U.C. position was sustained. Bevin's argument was that trade union negotiators could be relied upon to behave responsibly, and not to press inflationary demands. But he stressed that it was

---

[1] For a study of national wages policy in the Second World War, and the period immediately following, see B. C. Roberts, *National Wages Policy in War and Peace* (1958).

essential for them to retain the freedom to make claims in certain circumstances, for otherwise they would lose their authority over their memberships. Should this happen a wave of unofficial strikes could be expected, such as had characterised the First World War, and in that event the Government would be forced into making concessions, as it had then. Bevin felt the best way to deal with inflationary pressures was to act on prices; if these could be stabilised then it would be possible to stabilise wage rates also. The policy of self-government in industry was in fact justified by events. Inflation was kept within bounds, and any serious breakdown in industrial relations was avoided. There were, of course, unofficial strikes, and these reached a peak in 1943 and 1944 as the strain of wartime began to tell, but they never threatened to assume the same scale as those in the 1914–1918 conflict.

Citrine's policy in the war, as he made clear to the 1940 Congress was one of 'watchful but cordial collaboration' with the Government. But there was no question of the T.U.C. sacrificing its independence. As we have seen, Bevin, as Minister of Labour, understood this position, and encouraged it. He allowed the General Council a constructive role in the formation of policy in his own Ministry, and he defended the policy of voluntary co-operation against critics in the Cabinet. No one would pretend that relationships between him and Citrine were never strained during the war, for as individuals they had never got on well together. On matters of policy, however, they had nearly always shared a common viewpoint before the war, and this situation was not fundamentally changed when Bevin left the General Council to become Minister of Labour. Partly as a result of their influence the trade unions secured a degree of participation in the running of wartime industry that accorded well with their aspirations. Apart from its close relationship with the Ministry of Labour, the T.U.C. was involved in elaborate consultative machinery on the production side. It was represented along with the Employers' Federation on an Advisory Committee to the Minister of Production, and was also involved on an Industrial Panel which advised the Minister on specific problems. Finally, it was consulted on appointments that were made to the tripartite Regional Boards of the Ministry. Apart from the Ministry of Production, machinery also existed in connection with the Ministries of Supply, Aircraft, Admiralty and Fuel and Power.

It must be said, however, that relationships with the various Ministries were not always harmonious, as is made clear by the General Council's reports to the war time Congresses. Furthermore, it may be doubted whether the T.U.C. or its affiliated unions were always in a position to play a constructive role on the production side. In general the movement lacked the modern technical and economic research facilities which alone would have enabled it to give a lead on questions of production.[1] This was not surprising for, apart from anything else, British employers had not in the past encouraged the unions to trespass on 'managerial functions'. The great attraction behind the Mond–Turner talks had been the opportunity to expand the scope of union activity, and this opportunity the war certainly provided. Contact with the whole range of production problems was a valuable experience, and it was to greatly influence the thinking of Congress after 1945. There was one other form of consultation on the production side which deserves mention. This was the spontaneous wartime growth of Joint Production Committees at plant level. The T.U.C. in its nationalisation schemes of the 1930s had seen the necessity for consultation at plant level through Works Councils, and in this it was following the proposals of the Whitley Committee during the First World War. It now showed its approval of the Joint Production Committees, and a resolution was passed at the 1945 Congress recommending their permanent establishment in industry after the war. Apart from production, the T.U.C. interested itself in every aspect of wartime policy affecting labour, and on a wide range of issues its views were taken into account. For instance it set up a special Rationing and Price Committee, to consider matters relating to the supply of food and essential commodities, and at a local level the Trades Councils also took an interest in this problem. The wartime integration of the trade union movement into the economic life of the nation was complete.

2. RECONSTRUCTION – FOR WHOM?

The Second World War, like the First, stimulated the desire for change in society, and from early on in the conflict thoughts were directed to the problem of post-war reconstruction. Reconstruction was seen as an opportunity for reform in all the various aspects of

[1] See N. Barou, *British Trade Unions* (1947).

the national life, and the war years produced the Beveridge Report on Social Insurance in 1942, an Education Act in 1944, and a Government commitment to maintain full employment in peace time in the same year. Government thinking about reconstruction, like other aspects of its activity, was done in consultation with the unions, and the General Council Report for 1943 commented on the formation of a Reconstruction Joint Advisory Council, comprising the T.U.C., the employers and the Government. The T.U.C. produced its own Interim Report on Reconstruction in 1944. It cannot, however, be said that this document was of great significance in the development of trade-union policy, for it was virtually a restatement of the 1932 General Council Report on the Reorganisation of Industry. It envisaged an extension of public ownership, and of greater public regulation where industry remained in private hands. So far as control of nationalised undertakings was concerned, it adhered to the 1932 policy. Control should be in the hands of a Board to which appointments should be made on the basis of competence for the work. In so far as it was desirable to appoint at least some persons with a trade-union background, these persons should not act in a representative capacity, but should relinquish their posts in the union movement upon taking up the appointment. Recommendations regarding the creation of consultative machinery in socialised industries at national and workshop level followed almost exactly the 1932 statement. This organisational blueprint for nationalisation, which had been developed in consultation with the Labour Party during the thirties, was to form the basis of the Party's programme of public ownership when it took office in 1945. A further indication of continuity with the earlier period was the reappearance in the 1944 Report of the proposal to establish a National Industrial Council. Such a body 'would provide the Government with detailed industrial experience upon which to draw in the formulation of policy. It would also materially assist in the application of economic policy to industry'. These sentences might well have been taken out of the Mond–Turner Interim Report of 1928. The whole emphasis underlying the 1944 document was the claim that trade unions must be left to function independently in the post-war world. This underlies, of course, the N.I.C. proposal, with its emphasis on industrial self-government, but it is even more striking in relation to the proposals concerning public ownership. The main point about control of socialised undertakings was that trade union independence must be retained. If trade union officials were represented as such upon the Boards of these undertakings their independence and freedom of action would be compromised. The T.U.C. leadership held firmly to the view that independent labour organisation would be as necessary in socialised industry as in capitalist industry, and they were determined to resist any tendency for labour unions in Britain to become mere appendages of the state machine, as they were in the Soviet Union. As full workers' control was regarded as incompatible with industrial efficiency, it would be better for the unions to stay completely outside, and retain their freedom of action.

Quite apart from the question of publicly-owned undertakings, the 1944 Report made clear its wish that the voluntary principle should prevail over the whole industrial relations field:

We are bound to insist that in all circumstances Trade Unions should retain their present freedom from legal restraints upon their right to frame policy and pursue activities in support of that policy. . . . As voluntary associations of work people they must, in their policies, interpret the wishes of work people and their actions must be designed to protect in advance work people's common interests. Otherwise, though they may continue to exist as organisations, they will cease to be Trade Unions.

State intervention in industry had been growing steadily in the 1930s, and during the war the influence of Government became all-pervasive. This trend had been identified and welcomed by the T.U.C. in the early 1930s, but it was anxious above all in 1944 to mark off for itself and its affiliated unions a sphere of action independent of the state. Apart from the Reconstruction Report, the General Council Report to the 1944 Congress stressed in its introduction that while it had co-operated with the Government, it had maintained the independence of the trade-union movement. It will be recalled that Citrine had made a statement to the same effect at Congress four years before.

The claim made by the General Council that the movement should be free from control in the post-war world raised a good many issues. Trade-union membership expanded rapidly during the war, rising from 6,053,000 in 1938 to 7,803,000 in 1945. In 1946 it passed the previous record level of 8,000,000, attained briefly in 1920. The trade unions would thus be strong in the post-war world. Furthermore, given the commitment entered into by the Government to manage the economy so as to maintain a level of full employment, their strong bargaining power was likely to be maintained indefinitely. But strength was likely to bring responsibility, a responsibility to maintain economic stability in the new full employment situation, when the war was over and the imperatives for restraint were relaxed. Would the trade-union movement's plea for a free hand prove justifiable in these new circumstances? To some extent the answer to this question depended upon how the unions exercised their enhanced power, and whether they proved capable of conforming their policies to the national economic interest. This in turn raised the whole question of the internal structure of the movement, and its ability to adequately co-ordinate its activities, the very questions that had in very different circumstances preoccupied the founders of the General Council. The question of structure which had lain in abeyance during the 1930s had been raised again during the Second World War. In view of the generally radical temper of the times it was hardly surprising that Congress should have devoted some thought to its own reconstruction.

At the 1942 Congress a resolution was moved by F. J. Burrows of the N.U.R. in favour of an enquiry into structure. It was turned down by a fairly narrow majority. The tide of reconstruction was, however, running fast and in the following year Congress accepted a call for an investigation. Significantly, the resolution began: 'Congress, having in mind the still wider functions and responsibilities of the trade-union movement in the post-war period.' The General Council thus reopened the structural issue and by the time of the 1944 Blackpool Congress it had prepared an Interim Report. This document, like the Reconstruction Report of the same year, followed the lines of earlier thinking. The 1944 Interim Report was not an inspiring document. Of course, it can be argued that the reality of 962 overlapping and competing unions was not inspiring, and that the Council should be credited with facing up to this reality. Basically, the Report reaffirmed the viewpoint of the 1927 enquiry. Summarising the findings of that enquiry, the 1944 Report referred to 'the impossibility of such a body as the T.U.C., composed of all types of unions, reaching agreement on any specific form of organisation.' A reorganisation of structure was thus ruled out. 'It would be of no use the General

Council inviting unions to dismember themselves in order to conform to one or other theory of organisation.' What this meant in straightforward terms was that however desirable industrial unionism might be in theory, in practice it was ruled out by the existence of the powerful general unions. Given this fact the Report followed the 1927 policy in seeking ways, short of complete reorganisation, in which the movement could be adapted piecemeal to modern conditions. Amalgamations were recommended, emphasis was placed on the development of federations, and proposals were made for cutting down inter-union competition. Within the limits which it had set itself the Report was thorough enough, as had been that of 1927.

There was, however, an inherent contradiction about the whole exercise. For all the proposals for federation, amalgamation, and so on tacitly accepted the need for rationalisation on the basis of industry; as indeed had the T.U.C. reports on the nationalisation of coal, cotton and steel in the 1930s. Yet this tacit assumption could not be made explicit, the Report could not subscribe 'to one or other theory of organisation'. Following upon the Interim Report, which was accepted by Congress, the General Council conducted specific investigations into the situation in the various industries, and reports were produced each year, culminating in a final report in 1947. The recommendations were of course of the piecemeal character outlined in the Interim Report. So far as its own development was concerned, the T.U.C. made several suggestions. It suggested increasing the research and educational facilities provided by the Centre, and in connection therewith it was proposed to construct a new T.U.C. building. This proposal led ultimately to the building of Congress House – the present T.U.C. headquarters. So far as the role of the General Council as a co-ordinator of industrial policy was concerned, and this was surely extremely relevant to the post-war world, the Report returned to the original conception of the Council's creators – the Co-ordination Committee of 1919–21. It had then been proposed to forge a link between the various federations of unions and the Group Committees of the General Council. The Interim Report of 1944 admitted that the Group Committee system had never really functioned properly. The Council had, however, built up over the years a system of Advisory Committees covering various sectors of employment. There were such Committees covering non-manual workers, the nursing profession, local government, insurance, tobacco, women workers, engineering and ship building, while a Committee had existed in the mining industry during the thirties. Such Committees had, however, tended to cover sectors where particular problems of recruitment or demarcation were encountered, rather than forming a regular machinery for consultation between affiliated unions and the Centre. It was now proposed to extend the Advisory Committee system to each industry, and to associate the various federations with such Committees. In this way it was hoped to develop the contact of the General Council with industry on the lines originally envisaged in the 1921 reorganisation. Such hopes did not prove well founded.

The diligence of the T.U.C. in conducting the 1943–7 enquiry is not open to question, but the fact remains that the results achieved were limited in the extreme. The tidal wave of reconstruction (if such it may be called) left the trade-union movement, along with a number of other British institutions, untouched. After the war resolutions favouring structural change continued to appear before Congress, but the weight of the occupational and general unions was usually sufficient to block them. The General Secretary of the National Union of Public Employees, Bryn Roberts, an ardent exponent of industrial unionism, was moved to remark in 1950:

If the General Council rode up to Congress in a hansom cab, wearing bowlers and beards, it would be quite in keeping with our present day economic machinery.

As the post-war years went on the movement was increasingly to find itself criticised for its failure to modernise, so that by the latter half of the 1950s the high public esteem which the T.U.C. had won for itself in wartime had largely wasted away. The danger in this development was that public opinion might be less willing to admit that freedom of action and independence which Bevin and Citrine had valued so highly. However, quite apart from the external menace of legislation, there was also the fact that after 1948 total trade-union membership ceased to grow significantly, remaining for the next decade on a gently rising plateau. Bryn Roberts was to argue plausibly that stagnation in membership was a price the movement would have to pay for failing to undertake structural reform, for in the existing circumstances the General Council was inhibited from launching a really determined recruitment campaign for fear of revealing the underlying disunity and competitive character of the T.U.C.[1]

3. THE BURDENS OF OFFICE

Although the T.U.C. came under increasing criticism for failure to achieve modernisation as the post-war period developed, few at any rate could criticise the responsibility shown by General Council leaders during the critical economic situation in the first few years after the war. Before discussing this question, it is important to note that the composition of the T.U.C. leadership changed considerably after the war, partly as a result of the formation of a Labour Government in 1945 and its carrying through of a programme of public ownership. These developments resulted in the loss of a number of prominent T.U.C. figures to Government Service. Bevin, of course, had been outside the movement since 1940, and he became Foreign Secretary in the Labour Administration. His old place as Minister of Labour was filled by George Isaacs, who was General Council Chairman in 1945. It was, however, the nationalisation process which drew off many of the abler union leaders, and, as had been planned, labour appointees to Boards of Control in publicly owned undertakings resigned their former positions in the trade union movement. The most important loss was Citrine himself, who left the T.U.C. in 1946 to join the Coal Board and later became Chairman of the Electricity Authority. Other losses included Joseph Hallsworth of the Distributive Workers, a previous General Council Chairman, and James Bowman of the Miners, a particularly able man of the younger generation of leaders, both of whom went to the Coal Board. Bowman was thought by many to be the most promising young man on the General Council after the war, and his departure from the T.U.C. was much regretted.

The changes noted above resulted in a new pattern of T.U.C. leadership, that lasted from 1946 until 1955. A feature of the war and pre-war years had been the influence exerted upon the Congress by the General Secretary. After Citrine's departure in 1946 this situation changed. His successor as General Secretary was Vincent Tewson, a Yorkshireman, who had joined the T.U.C. staff a year after Citrine, in 1925. He began as Secretary of the newly

[1] Bryn Roberts, *The Price of T.U.C. Leadership* (1961).

formed Organisation Department. Six years later, when Alec Firth, Assistant Secretary, left the T.U.C. Tewson took his place and there he remained as Citrine's principal lieutenant for the next fifteen years. In October 1946 his succession to Citrine was unopposed. For all his other qualities, Tewson was not a man to give a strong personal lead to the movement, and during his ten years of office effective leadership was exercised by a group of powerful union leaders on the General Council. The General Secretary of the T.U.C. no longer set the tone for the whole movement, as Citrine had done; he executed the policies of the dominant group on the Council. What mattered in the immediate post-war situation, however, was that such a dominant group did in fact exist. For its existence enabled the General Council to give a strong lead to the trade-union movement. So far as immediate economic policy was concerned, there was at least a consensus at the centre.

The quartet which together with Vincent Tewson exercised leadership after 1946 was composed of Arthur Deakin, General Secretary of the T.G.W.U., Sir William Lawther, President of the Miners, Tom Williamson, General Secretary of the National Union of General and Municipal Workers, and Lincoln Evans, General Secretary of the Iron and Steel Trades Confederation. Between them they could mobilise about one-third of the votes at Congress. Given the support of a number of medium-sized unions, they were therefore in a position to determine Congress policy. The most influential figure in the group was Arthur Deakin, a forceful character who had served a long apprenticeship as Assistant General Secretary to Ernest Bevin in the T.G.W.U.[1] Although hardly of Bevin's calibre, Deakin was an able man, and like Bevin he was prepared to use his position as Secretary of Britain's largest union to give a strong lead on general policy issues. In the history of the General Council, only Bramley, Bevin and Citrine can be said to have exercised a more important role than Arthur Deakin. It is time now to examine the direction which his leadership took in the immediate post-war world.

Britain's economic position at the end of the war was critical. Nothing had been spared in the war effort, and this had meant, among other things, a complete neglect of the export trade. It was clear that when the war was over, and the economy was adjusted to peacetime requirements, high priority would have to be given

[1] For a study of Arthur Deakin see V. L. Allen, *Trade Union Leadership* (1957).

to exports in order to pay for those supplies of food and raw materials on which the nation depended. Furthermore, the war had depleted Britain's sources of invisible earnings, thus placing an even greater emphasis on the need to produce for export. These considerations weighed heavily with the Labour Government that took office in 1945, and in the period until 1950 it ran the economy on the assumption that private consumption at home would have to be curbed in order to make way for exports and investment. The latter was necessary in order to raise the productive capacity of industry. This situation placed a heavy responsibility upon the trade-union movement, as we shall see below, but it was one which the General Council of the T.U.C. was prepared to accept. Deakin and his associates were prepared to co-operate, partly out of loyalty to a Labour Government as such, but also because they accepted the Government's diagnosis of the economic situation and the ways in which it could be met. Furthermore the general policy of the Labour Government, in its implementation of a public-ownership programme and particularly in its expansion of the social services, was in accord with established T.U.C. policy. Finally, the Attlee Government was successful in maintaining full employment throughout the first five years of peace. This was a blessing which trade-union leaders did not underestimate.

The T.U.C. leadership accepted responsibility for trade-union conduct in two major fields, production and wages. The imperative to produce more was almost as great in the first five years of peace as it had been in wartime. In this situation the General Council agreed that Order 1305, prohibiting strikes, should be continued, and in fact it remained in operation until 1951. Various other war-time restrictions in industry were also continued after 1945 with the concurrence of the T.U.C. leadership. Order No. 1305 would, however, have been unenforceable had it not been backed by the voluntary determination of the trade-union leaders to avoid any disruption of the production drive. In March 1946 the General Council, at the request of the Government, called a conference of executives to London to enable Ministers to explain to the move-ment the economic problems the country faced. The Council itself remained in close contact with the various economic Ministries, and was represented on the National Production Advisory Council on Industry, a body chaired by Sir Stafford Cripps as President of the Board of Trade. The General Council acted continuously to interpret and explain Government policies and problems, and threw its weight behind appeals for increased production. The unions were in the main prepared to respond to this lead, as was shown at the 1947 Congress, where several resolutions concerned themselves with proposals for better methods and great efficiency in industry. In the following year the Council's involvement in production problems was taken even further, and it convened a special conference of trade-union executives in November 1948. The conference accepted, almost without opposition, the General Council report on productivity, which made various suggestions as to the avoidance of waste in manpower and equipment, and commented on the obstacles raised to greater efficiency by restrictive practices on both sides of industry. The report also favoured greater use of joint consultation in industry, as a means to higher productivity. The Joint Production Committees tended to disappear after the war, and the T.U.C. leadership strongly favoured their revival. In October 1948 Stafford Cripps and Paul G. Hoffman of the United States created the Anglo-American Council on Productivity, and the General Council became actively involved on this body. Lincoln Evans, the Council's spokesman on economic matters, became Joint Chairman of the British section, Vincent Tewson the Joint Secretary, and Arthur Deakin and Will Lawther among others were also members of the British section. T.U.C. support for the productivity drive continued through 1949 and 1950. A team was sent to the United States 'to study the part played by American trade unions in the achieving and maintaining of the high average rate of industrial productivity operating in the U.S.A.' The team recommended on its return that in Britain the larger unions and federations should establish production engineering departments and train production engineers, and that the T.U.C. should have a staff able both to assist the setting up of such departments and to provide direct services where unions were too small to engage their own staff.[1] To what extent these developments would be feasible without structural reorganisation was, of course, a question.

On the issue of increased production after the war the willingness of the General Council to co-operate with the Labour Government was never in doubt. Its co-operation was absolute, and because in this era the General Council's influence over affiliated

[1] T.U.C., *Trade Unions and Productivity* (1950).

unions was very strong, T.U.C. co-operation counted for a lot. The other major issue was wages. On wages the attitude of the T.U.C. was much less positive. To suggestions that the Government might introduce controls over wages, Arthur Deakin at first responded, as Bevin had done in 1940, with violent opposition, stating that he would prefer to see the direction of labour reintroduced. The Government, as in wartime, respected the voluntary system of collective bargaining, and this had been made clear by George Isaacs, the Minister of Labour, in 1946. However, given the full-employment situation, there was a danger of wage increases leading to higher costs in industry, which would affect the export drive. The unions were therefore called upon, as during the war, to exercise a voluntary wage restraint. The General Council was reluctant to support the Government on this issue, as it was doing on that of production, but its hand was forced by the publication in February 1948 of a White Paper on Personal Incomes Costs and Prices, on which there had been no prior consultation. The General Council had, of course, no power to bind affiliated unions to a policy of wage restraint, but it decided to seek to obtain a commitment to the policy by convening a conference of union executives and pressing the individual unions to accept its view. Such conferences were becoming a regular part of the post-war scene, as the General Council, in its desire to actively influence policy in industry, strove to overcome its limitations as an executive body. Thus on 24 March 1948 executive committee members of affiliated unions crowded into the Central Hall Westminster to hear the Council's plea for an endorsement of the Government's policy of wage restraint. The Council's report pointed out that the Labour Government had adopted and applied the T.U.C.'s industrial policy, and had implemented this policy in constant consultation with the T.U.C. 'It is unthinkable', the report commented, 'that we in the Trade Union Movement should now stand on one side and ignore the request the Government has made to us'. The delegates accepted the Council's report by 5,421,000 votes to 2,032,000. The wage restraint policy was legally observed, but the limitations on wage increases came too late to prevent the balance of payments from worsening to a degree that made devaluation impossible to avoid. In 1949 Stafford Cripps, now Chancellor of the Exchequer, asked the General Council to tighten up its wages policy as a result of the devaluation crisis in that year, and in December 1949 the Council produced a report reaffirming its acceptance of wage restraint. It made, however, three reservations. Firstly, there must be no Government imposition of a wages policy – the voluntary system must be preserved. Secondly, the T.U.C. itself could not impose a wages policy upon affiliated unions, although it had a right to expect that they would conform to policies that had been democratically endorsed. Finally, the Council could not agree to a complete standstill on wages: there would be a need for a review of the lowest wages, and there ought to be prospects for wage increases in line with productivity increases. A further conference of executives followed on 12 January 1950 in which the General Council again put the case for wage restraint, with the reservations noted above. This time, however, its report was accepted only by a narrow majority. The policy was due to come for review again at the end of the year. However, the 1950 Congress passed a resolution against the General Council, stating its opposition to further restraint. T.U.C.-sponsored wage restraint was thus at an end. Within limits the policy had been effective while it had lasted, but it had run into increasing opposition from the rank and file of the unions, and the rise in the cost of living during 1950, as the Korean War made its impact, was the final blow.

The efforts of Deakin and his associates on the General Council to secure the backing of the unions for increased production and wage restraint had not been assisted by international developments at the end of the 1940s. Between 1941, when Russia had joined the war against Germany, and 1947, when the 'cold war' began, Communism ceased to provoke the hostility of the official movement, as the Communists gave their backing to the unions' co-operation in raising production. Although the majority of the General Council continued to hold the British Communist Party and its followers in contempt, they saw in the wartime co-operation with Russia the hope that the pre-war conflict with the Red Trade Union International would be brought to an end. Discussions with the Russians began and agreement was reached on the creation of a World Federation of Trade Unions, which was launched in Paris in 1945. The Federation included, in addition to the Russian and British movements, the chief Continental European trade-union centres and the American Congress of Industrial Organisations. The other American body, the American Federation of Labour, with whom the British movement had had close contacts since 1894, refused to join. The creation of the W.F.T.U. owed a good deal to T.U.C. efforts, and Citrine became its first President. When Citrine left the union movement, his place at the head of the Federation was taken by Arthur Deakin. The split between East and West, however, wrecked the W.F.T.U. within a short time of its birth, and in 1949 the T.U.C., C.I.O., and other Western trade-union centres withdrew to form their own International Confederation of Free Trade Unions. In 1951 Vincent Tewson became President of this new body. The renewed split between Communist and non-Communist in the international movement was reflected in the domestic British scene, where subversive activities once more became an issue at the T.U.C. In view of the General Council's strong commitment in support of the Government's economic policy, it reacted vigorously against Communist attempts to mobilise the rank and file in resistance to increased production and wage restraint. In 1948 it urged affiliated unions to ban Communists from office, and Deakin, who was waging a battle in his own union to prevent the Communists from taking control, secured a change of rules which prevented Communists from holding office as full-time officials. The Communist menace in the late forties was no illusion, for party members secured complete control of a few unions, and obtained important posts in others. Furthermore, at local level, they were a force encouraging resort to unofficial strikes, such as developed in the port industry at the close of the decade. However, while Communism undoubtedly presented an obstacle to the fulfilment of the T.U.C's policy, it would be incorrect to blame it for the ending of wage restraint. The General Council had been successful in securing support for wage restraint for a period of about two years. Such a policy could not have been operated for much longer under the voluntary system, especially given the rising cost of living, without completely alienating the union leaderships from the rank and file. By 1950 the population of Great Britain were ready for an end to the austerity that had been their lot for nearly a decade.

F

4. THE LOSS OF DIRECTION

In 1951 Labour lost the General Election and a Conservative Administration took over. For the moment, this political development did not bring any decisive change in the affairs of the T.U.C. The General Council announced its readiness to work amicably with the new Government. This statement aroused a good deal of criticism on the left wing of the movement, the more so when the Conservatives began to de-nationalise the iron and steel industry. The Council were, however, not making any break with the past in affirming their readiness to co-operate with a non-Labour Government. Back in 1938 Citrine had justified the Council's dealings with the Chamberlain Government, on the grounds that the T.U.C. was an industrial organisation, and so it was in 1951. Furthermore the Minister of Labour in the new Government, Sir Walter Monckton, showed himself ready to co-operate with the unions, and the consultative machinery inherited from the previous administration was continued under the new. The continued high standing of the T.U.C. with the Government, despite the transition from Labour to Conservative rule, indicated the extent to which the movement had become virtually part of the establishment. To run through the list of leading T.U.C. figures is not unlike running through a list of leading Civil Servants: Sir Vincent Tewson, Sir William Lawther, Sir Thomas Williamson, Sir Lincoln Evans. As Churchill once remarked, the trade-union movement had become the Fourth Estate of the realm. The Conservative regime proved to be more permissive in economic terms than its predecessor: controls were removed, private consumption given more rein, and wages allowed to rise. To what extent this permissiveness was purchased at a long-term cost in economic growth is a matter for argument. Certainly the new order of things placed much less responsibility on the T.U.C. leadership, at least for the time being. The Government relied largely on demand management in running the economy, and the questions of incomes policy or direct action to improve productivity in industry received little emphasis. After 1955, when the Conservatives were again returned, the economy increasingly ran into balance of payments difficulties and very slowly the Government began to move back towards more intervention in industry, a tendency which would once more bring calls for T.U.C. responsibility and co-operation. An observer in 1956 might well have doubted however whether, under the new circumstances, such co-operation would be forthcoming.

The positive role played by the T.U.C. between 1945 and 1950, in recovery from the war, had been possible in part because the Government of the day enjoyed the full confidence of the trade-union leadership. This was bound to be less the case after 1951 and even more after 1955, following the Conservatives' somewhat obvious use of the Budget for electoral purposes. But this was not the only problem. The strength of the lead given by the General Council in the earlier period resulted not from any constitutional power it possessed over affiliated unions, but because a clique of leaders existed who were sufficiently powerful to dominate Congress policy. The quartet of Deakin, Lawther, Evans and Williamson could not, however, survive indefinitely, even if it was desirable that it should. Deakin, much the most important figure of the group, died in 1955. When Frank Cousins became General Secretary of the T.G.W.U. the following year all cohesion on the General Council vanished, for his left-wing views were in marked contrast to those of the other members of the group. There had been some aspects of the Deakin regime which had been unsatisfactory, and these had become particularly marked during the early fifties. The dominance of the occupational and general unions ruled out the possibility of reorganisation in the movement, and this was a serious handicap, for inter-union conflicts did much to tarnish the public image of the trade unions after 1950. But the grouping which Deakin led had provided a degree of cohesion which the T.U.C. lacked after 1955. It had been a substitute for greater General Council powers, but, in the forties at any rate, it had been a fairly effective substitute. Now that it was gone the vacuum at the centre stood revealed. Given the status of the unions in society, and their crucial role in a full-employment situation, it was a vacuum which would have to be filled. If it was not filled effectively the country would suffer as well as the trade unions. The election of George Woodcock as General Secretary in 1960 was hailed by all those who believed that the T.U.C. ought to give a vigorous and positive leadership to the trade-union movement, wiping out the image of the famous cartoonist Low who always depicted the T.U.C. as a massive old carthorse, plodding steadily along, but incapable of getting up a gallop or taking a fence in show jumper style. Woodcock had all the qualifications for a brilliant success. A Lancashire weaver, who had started work as a lad and then gone to Ruskin College at the age of twenty-five, afterwards going on to New College to take a first-class honours degree in politics, philosophy and economics. After a short spell as a civil servant, he had been selected by Citrine to succeed Milne-Bailey as head of the Research Department. He thus brought to the job the advantages of considerable reputation for intellectual ability, deep roots in the trade-union movement, a training by Citrine, and experience of working at the T.U.C. for twenty-five years. Here perhaps was his weakness, he had never led a trade union and some members of the General Council might not be able to overlook this fact. Perhaps his greatest problem, however, lay in his own personality and philosophy. Woodcock, as he put it himself on one occasion, was a reactionary – he did not really believe in initiating new developments, he preferred to react to other people's proposals and to situations. He saw the trade-union movement as the working man's inevitable response to the challenge of industrialism; its form was shaped not by an intellectual process of positive decisions, but gradually by experience in the fullness of time. A cynic by nature, a moralist by inclination, with a personality compounded of shyness and arrogance, Woodcock was called upon to lead the trade unions at a time when action as well as reaction was the critical requirement. The way in which he has sought to make the unions aware of the choice before them is an important part of the last chapter of this history of the T.U.C.

9 The Challenge of Change, 1957-68

I. THE CONTEMPORARY SITUATION

DURING the last decade of the century of its existence the T.U.C. has been dominated by the problem of coming to terms with rapidly changing economic, social and political conditions. The role of the T.U.C. in contemporary Britain is of immense significance; no national institution is in a position of greater social importance. The contribution to the welfare of society which the T.U.C. has the opportunity to make cannot be overrated, yet in spite of its supremely important role, the power it represents and the fact that there lies behind it a hundred years of remarkable achievement, the T.U.C. begins its second century of life under a question mark.

That a Royal Commission on Trade Unions should report as the T.U.C. celebrates its hundredth year of existence is a remarkable twist of fate, since it was the establishment of the Royal Commission whose reports laid the foundation of the industrial relations system which has prevailed over this period, more than any other factor, that led to the first meeting of the T.U.C. in Manchester in 1868. The fundamental issue before the Royal Commission on Trade Unions and Employers Associations, which reported in 1968 has been the extent to which the system of industrial relations established by its predecessor one hundred years ago requires to be changed.

The principles endorsed by the Royal Commission of 1867-9 included the recognition of the right of workpeople to organise and join unions, to bargain collectively and to strike with the minimum of legal constraint. The system of industrial relations built up on this voluntary basis is uniquely British – no other system of industrial relations anywhere in the world operates with less reliance on the law – it is believed by trade unionists, perhaps not so fervently by employers, to be the best system of industrial relations in the world. *Laissez-faire* collectivism, as the system has been termed, worked tolerably well up to the end of the

Second World War, but since then it has increasingly been called in question. The establishment of the Royal Commission was final confirmation that the system was not proving adequate to meet the needs of a modern society.

Under contemporary conditions, the British system of industrial relations has not met the need to produce a pattern of wages and salaries that has been compatible with the maintenance of relatively stable prices; nor one that has induced high levels of productivity or achieved a distribution of income between occupational and social groups that is accepted as reasonably equitable either to the lowest paid workers or to those in technical, professional and managerial jobs. It is also clear from Britain's position at the bottom of the economic growth league that when tested against the need to facilitate economic and technological change the industrial relations system has not been working efficiently. The function of an industrial relations system is to smooth out the human and organisational conflicts that inevitably arise when change takes place, but the growth of unofficial strikes and the relatively large number of work stoppages that are occurring is evidence that the system has not adjusted to meet the stresses that are now arising.

As the deficiencies in the British system of industrial relations had become increasingly obvious it was no surprise when in 1964 the newly elected Labour Government decided to appoint a Royal Commission on Trade Unions and Employers' Associations to report on 'relations between management and employees, and the role of trade unions and employers' associations in promoting the interests of their members and in accelerating the social and economic advance of the nation with particular reference to the law affecting the activities of these institutions'. There can be no doubt that significant changes will have to be made and almost all of those considered by the Royal Commission have important implications for the Trades Union Congress. None more so than in the field of incomes policy.

2. A TRADE-UNION INCOMES POLICY

In the last twenty-odd years Britain has successfully maintained a high general level of employment. There have been fluctuations in the demand for labour leading from time to time to situations when the number of jobs available exceeded the number of people looking for work, and at other times to more unemployed than vacancies to be filled. But these fluctuations in the employment level have been small compared with those that used to occur. There have also been marked differences in the levels of unemployment in different regions making for problems of mobility for both labour and capital, but here again great improvements have been secured compared with the situation that existed before the Second World War, when some areas almost died from lack of economic activity.

No objective has been rated more important by the trade unions than the maintenance of full employment. In its evidence to the Royal Commission on Trade Unions and Employers' Associations the T.U.C. stated that 'Trade Unionists see full employment as an end in itself, but also as a necessary means to achieving consistently rising national prosperity'. However, the problem that the trade unions have found extremely hard to face squarely is that the traditional methods of collective bargaining give rise to difficulties under conditions of full employment that make the maintenance of full employment incompatible with the maintenance of stable prices and a favourable balance of payments situation.

The problem was pointed out in the discussion during the Second World War on whether the maintenance of full employment ought to be accepted by the Government as a specific goal of economic policy. In the years that have since elapsed experience has amply confirmed that under full employment, trade unions and employers will always fix wages, salaries and profits at levels that exceed the rate of economic growth in real terms. The chronic tendency for this to happen has been one of the major factors in the persistent adverse balance of payments situation from which the British economy has suffered during the post-war period. The problem of restraining the growth of incomes so as to prevent inflation has been made more difficult by the rate of increase in public expenditure and on the other side of the equation the failure of productivity to rise at a more rapid pace. However, even if public expenditure had been more carefully controlled and output had gone up faster, the fundamental problem of maintaining an equilibrium between the rate of rise of money incomes and the rate of rise of output would still remain.

Although Britain has fallen to the bottom of the economic

growth league during the post-war period, it is apparent from the experience of other countries – even including Japan which has had an average growth of almost 10 per cent a year over the last decade compared with Britain's 3 per cent – that high growth rates will not by themselves prevent incomes from rising even faster if institutional circumstances make this possible.

It is now recognised almost everywhere that unregulated collective bargaining is likely to push wage and salary costs upwards and so lead to price increases with consequential effects on every part of the economic system. In 1948 when the T.U.C. persuaded the conference of trade union executives to accept the policy of wage restraint, it did so merely as a temporary concession to a passing need arising out of the peculiar difficulties that were being encountered after more than five years of total war. The unions did not accept the logic of economists who pointed out the inescapable consequences that would follow if incomes were pushed up at a faster pace than the output of the economy.

The attitude of the unions was also shared by most employers and political parties. However, by 1960 it was becoming apparent to the Conservatives that it was extremely difficult to check inflation by traditional monetary and budgetary methods without creating economic recessions that involved levels of unemployment that could have an almost certainly disastrous political consequence for the party in power. The change in the attitude of the Conservative Party towards collective bargaining was influenced by two other factors. One was the failure of Mr. Frank Cousins, whose London Busmen were out on strike for seven weeks in 1958, without success, the T.U.C. refusing to come to their aid by bringing out on strike members of other unions. This event was seen by the Government as evidence supporting the case for taking a stronger line with the unions and this was especially significant, since in the previous year when the engineering employers had stood up to the striking engineering unions they had been encouraged by the Ministry of Labour to settle on terms which were evidently inflationary.

Even more important, however, was the change in the intellectual climate of opinion about the nature of the inflationary process. This shift was made manifest in the striking difference between the first and last report of the Council on Prices, Productivity and Incomes. The Council had been set up in 1957 and its first report had come to the conclusion that inflation was primarily caused by excess demand and not by trade union bargaining strength. It suggested that the over-rapid rise in wages could be checked by appropriate fiscal and monetary measures that would allow the unemployment level to rise above the very low average which had prevailed in the previous post-war years. This report was vigorously denounced by the T.U.C. as a vicious attack on full employment and workers' living standards. The T.U.C., thereafter, refused to co-operate with the Council. The last Report of the Council shifted the emphasis from 'demand pull' to 'cost push' as the decisive factor in the inflationary spiral. It saw little advantage in deflationary remedies and stressed the need for a 'guiding light' and positive investment and incomes planning. This view was apparently more acceptable to T.U.C. leaders, even though its policy implications pointed towards limitations on the freedom to bargain.

The Government sought to avoid a head-on conflict with the trade unions, but faced by a balance of payments crisis in July 1961, they were convinced that in addition to a credit squeeze, they had to try to influence the actual settlement of levels of pay by themselves giving a decisive lead. They, therefore, inaugurated a 'pay pause' for civil servants and public employees. The theory behind this policy, which had been vigorously advanced by a number of Conservative back-bench Members of Parliament, was based on the quite erroneous belief that the Government as an employer was the leader of the annual wage round, and, therefore, the main culprit responsible for setting inflationary levels of pay increases. Unfortunately for the Government, this policy soon foundered on public hostility towards the 'pay pause' which saw it as a mean attempt to make hapless nurses and teachers bear the brunt of responsibility for inflation.

The Government's 'pay pause' policy came in for bitter criticism at the annual Congress of the T.U.C. It was attacked not only because it had been introduced without prior consultation, but also because it interfered with the freedom of collective bargaining. Warnings were uttered by the unions that they would take drastic steps if the Government did not abandon what they considered to be an outrageously discriminatory policy against workers in public employment.

At the beginning of the New Year, the Union of Post Office

Workers began a work to rule protest against the rejection of its pay claim. This was followed by the Post Office Engineering Union, and the Civil Service Clerical Association threatened to follow suit. Soon afterwards, it was announced that the 'pay pause' would end on 31 March 1962.

At the same time as the Government was seeking to hold wage increases in check, it moved to establish a National Economic Development Council, composed of representatives of the unions, employers, nationalised industries, public members and representatives of the Government. The General Council of the T.U.C. looked with favour on this development, but it would not agree to joining if the N.E.D.C. was to be responsible for administering a policy of wage restraint to which it would be committed. The Government accepted this reservation of the T.U.C. and decided to establish a separate National Incomes Commission.

Before the 'pay pause' came to an end, the Government issued a White Paper, *Incomes Policy: The Next Step*, setting out the criteria by which wage increases ought in future to be judged. It followed closely a report on wages which had been presented to the President of the United States by the Council of Economic Advisers. The Government had already indicated to the T.U.C. that during the year wages should not normally exceed a 'guiding light' of $2\frac{1}{2}$ per cent.

These ideas for restraining wages were looked upon by the trade unions with acute suspicion. The 'guiding light' was in fact widely ignored; the T.U.C. refused to recognise the existence of the National Incomes Commission and advised member organisations against co-operation with it. Nevertheless, in spite of the refusal of the T.U.C. to co-operate with a Conservative Government in the administration of an incomes policy, speeches by leaders of the Labour Party indicated that if the Party was returned to power at the next election an incomes policy would be an essential ingredient of its recipe for curing Britain of its economic disease.

By this time, Reginald Maudling, the Conservative Chancellor, was ready to accept the arguments advanced by the T.U.C. and an important section of intellectual opinion that the only way to obtain union support and to get the economy operating at a faster growth rate without running into balance of payments crisis, was to break out of the 'stop-go' cycle. The policy of reflation introduced by the Chancellor worked extremely quickly and the economy roared ahead, but though the General Council indicated, in its policy statement to the 1963 Congress, that it recognised the need for some wage restraint it was not prepared to take any steps to make such a policy effective.

By the middle of 1964 the boom had led to a run on the pound and a serious deficit position was rapidly building up. The attempt to avoid dampening down the economy in the hope that productivity would overtake the rise in incomes had failed and with it the long period of Conservative rule. Home demand had driven up costs and left no room for exports to expand as required. The defeat of the Conservatives brought the Labour Party back into office in the autumn of 1964. The new Government, faced by a large balance of payments deficit, rejected devaluation as a way out of the economic crisis and set about the task of developing a long-term national economic plan and an incomes policy supported by the unions.

The T.U.C. General Council recognised the task in front of the Government, but it was not easily persuaded that it should join with the C.B.I. and the Government in making a Declaration of Intent on Productivity, Prices and Incomes. In this public state-ment the Government undertook to introduce a national economic plan in consultation with the trade unions and the employers, and the T.U.C. and C.B.I. in their turn agreed to co-operate in the establishment of a prices and incomes policy.

The T.U.C. was by no means entirely satisfied with the decision of the Government to establish a Department of Economic Affairs embracing much of the work that had hitherto been carried out by the National Economic Development Council. Nor were they completely convinced that an independent National Board for Prices and Incomes as proposed by the Government, was the most suitable type of machinery to establish to administer the prices and incomes policy.

However, a White Paper on the policy the Prices and Incomes Board would follow, and some vigorous lobbying by the Secretary of State for Economic Affairs, persuaded the General Council to call a meeting of trade-union executives to consider supporting the policies outlined by the Government. Mr. George Woodcock was clearly unhappy at being precipitously pushed along by Mr. George Brown, and though he supported the development of a national incomes policy, he believed that this could only be achieved gradually.

There was considerable opposition to the acceptance of the proposed incomes policy, led by Mr. Clive Jenkins, General Secretary of the Association of Supervisory Staffs, Executives and Technicians, and from the Transport and General Workers' Union, whose General Secretary, Mr. Frank Cousins, had joined the Government. The vote in favour of supporting the policy advocated by the General Council was eventually carried by 6,649,000 to 1,811,000, at the meeting of trade union executives.

In the event, wages rose considerably faster than the 3½ per cent norm which had been laid down as the permissible limit. Faced by the continued tendency for wages to go up too quickly, the Government decided to seek powers to secure and enforce an early warning system of price and pay increases and to defer any such increases until the Prices and Incomes Board had examined and reported on them. The T.U.C. and the C.B.I. were uneasy at this development, which they feared might be the thin end of the wedge, leading to a statutory enforcement of a comprehensive price and pay policy. However, the General Council decided not to oppose the Government's plans, but to develop its own wage claim vetting policy which would make it unnecessary for the Government to activate the compulsory early warning and delaying powers.

Opposition to the Government's incomes policy was defeated by a substantial majority at the annual Congress in 1965, but the voluntary vetting policy was only carried by the relatively narrow majority of 1·9 million. The plain fact was that many unions were extremely reluctant, as they had always been, to accept either Government or T.U.C. control over their right to bargain. Most trade union members and their leaders simply refused to recognise that the economic situation demanded a fundamental change in the traditional collective bargaining system.

The vetting system was put into effect a few weeks after the 1965 Congress and during the next nine months some 600 wage claims were examined by a Wage Policy Committee made up of one member from each of the 19 trade groups from which the Council is composed. The Committee let most of the claims through – though most of them were generally considerably in excess of any norm that would have been non-inflationary. The Committee was often inadequately informed as to the cost consequences of the increases wanted and no attempt was made to probe deeply into any claim. But the greatest weakness of the efforts of the T.U.C. was that it refused to insist on any non-inflationary norm being followed. The Prices and Incomes Board followed a much tougher line, but its effect overall was relatively slight and wage rates rose from mid-1965 to mid-1966 by almost 8 per cent and hourly earnings by 10 per cent.

The balance of payments had shown some improvement, but the situation was suddenly seriously and adversely influenced by a seamen's strike which lasted forty-seven days. The effect of this strike, on a precarious situation, was disastrous; it led to a run on the already extremely weak pound and it led finally to a settlement which burst through the incomes policy by pushing up shipping labour costs by 10 per cent. In July the Government was again compelled to introduce crisis measures, including a general price and incomes freeze. The trade unions had no liking for this policy, but with the high hopes of the national plan now shattered and the Government compelled to introduce severe deflationary measures to save the pound, the T.U.C. was in no position to prevent the Government passing a Prices and Incomes Act containing a compulsory early warning system and powers to impose a standstill on prices and incomes until the end of 1966. They were, however, able to persuade the Government to limit the Act to a period of twelve months only.

The General Council still clung to the view that a voluntary incomes policy could only be achieved gradually and feared that 'such short-run effects as a freeze might produce might, therefore, be purchased at the cost of a long-term agreement on the need for a more rational method of relating the rise in incomes as a whole to the rise in productivity'. The dilemma before the General Council lay in its fear that if it refused to continue to help the Government by making the T.U.C. policy more effective, this might compel the Government to introduce further statutory controls, or else resort to more deflation and a higher level of unemployment.

At the 1966 Congress, in spite of the fact that the Prime Minister addressed the delegates himself and explained exactly why the Government had found it necessary to introduce the pay and price standstill, opposition to the Council's support for the incomes policy was considerable. A resolution against the compulsory early warning system was only defeated by 4,683,000 votes to 4,209,000. Another resolution declaring the outright opposition of the Congress to the pay freeze and the Prices and Incomes Act was defeated by a rather larger majority, but it was supported by almost four million votes.

The divisions in the voting at the Congress clearly revealed the limited support enjoyed by the General Council for the policy it was pursuing. The Council was in fact quite unable to prevent A.S.S.E.T. and other unions from using every means possible to make a breach in the Government's policy, and the Government was compelled to invoke its compulsory powers shortly after the Congress was over.

In October 1966 the General Council decided to undertake a comprehensive review of future incomes policy in relation to the achievement of a planned economic growth. A statement was issued by the General Council in November which gave more positive support for the development of a long-term incomes policy than ever before. The statement attempted to spell out in general terms the conditions under which the T.U.C. might successfully co-operate with the Government in the administration of a national incomes policy. It proposed that the vetting procedure which had been suspended during the period of the standstill should be reintroduced during the period of severe restraint which was to follow. Thereafter, the General Council would, it suggested, issue towards the end of each year an annual report on the economic situation and an estimate of prospects for the ensuing year. The Council would give its views on the general level of increase in wages and salaries that the economy could sustain and the circumstances under which any deviations from the general norm might be permitted. This report would be drawn up after consultation with the Department of Economic Affairs and the C.B.I., but solely on the responsibility of the General Council. The report would then be put to a meeting of trade-union executives and, if endorsed, would thereafter guide the Council in its examination of claims and settlements notified to it under the vetting scheme which would be extended in its scope.

These steps would constitute the Council claimed 'a significant advance towards a co-ordinated trade union incomes policy'. The proposals of the General Council were considered at a special meeting of trade-union executives in March, and endorsed by a majority of 7,604,000 votes to 963,000. This decision aroused great optimism, since it seemed to provide the basis for the development and administration of an autonomous incomes policy. In the opinion of the General Secretary of the T.U.C. this would make it unnecessary for the Government to continue its emergency legislation to control the fixing of pay. The Government was not, however, convinced that it could rely on the T.U.C. and it had to face the problem of preventing wages and salaries from rising rapidly when its present powers lapsed and before the T.U.C. scheme had started.

Following discussions with the T.U.C. and the C.B.I., the Government issued a White Paper in March 1967 outlining the criteria that should determine prices and incomes after the end of the period of severe restraint and the nil-norm. The White Paper stated that the Government wished to create conditions favourable to sustained economic growth and to avoid the stop-go cycle; and to work as quickly as possible towards the operation of an effective voluntary policy in agreement with the T.U.C. and the C.B.I. Since the part of the Prices and Incomes Act 1966 which gave the Government power to freeze the payment of increases in wages that were in breach of the standstill would lapse on 11 August 1967, it was necessary for the Government to take powers to impose a delay in the implementation of pay or price increases that were notified to the National Board for Prices and Incomes. The T.U.C. was not very keen on a new act, but the Government regarded further legislation as essential and the Prices and Incomes Act that came into effect on 12 August 1967, gave the Government power to impose delays of up to seven months on increases in prices, charges, wages and salaries.

At the 1967 Trades Union Congress considerable hostility was again voiced at the Government's economic policy. A motion was carried deploring 'the use by the Government of traditional deflationary measures to manage the economy which involve the creation of a pool of unemployed' and rejecting 'the Government's intervention in collective bargaining as a solution to the country's economic problems'. In spite of a powerful plea from Mr. George Woodcock, the General Secretary, asking Congress to oppose this motion, it was carried by a majority of 1,381,000. Congress also defeated a motion supporting the Government's incomes policy, while passing another that stated that 'the Prices and Incomes

Acts have been detrimental to the best interests of trade unionists and calls for their repeal'.

The mood of the majority of the members of Congress was clearly growing more hostile to the idea of a national incomes policy. There was little appreciation of the economic crisis that was beginning to blow up once again. Pressure on the pound, due to the failure of the balance of payments to recover and signs of continuing inflation, was increased when shortly after Congress had ended an unofficial dock strike started in London. The strike was against the decasualisation of dock work in the Port of London which had just been introduced.

In a healthy economic situation the dock strike would have been little more than a passing irritation, but in the convalescent state of the pound, it was a tremendous setback to international confidence. The situation steadily worsened until the Government had no choice but to accept devaluation. This decision had looked inevitable for a considerable time and it could only have been avoided by much sterner deflationary policies, or by an effective incomes policy; the T.U.C. and the Government will not be prepared to take the steps necessary to achieve either.

In the light of devaluation and the still precarious balance-of-payments situation, the first of the T.U.C.'s new-style economic reports and the incomes policy proposals that the special meeting of trade-union executive was to be asked to endorse on February 28, seemed highly optimistic. The analysis of the economic situation was penetrating and persuasive and the positive proposals had considerable merit as a finely calculated effort to win the support of the trade unions. However, insofar as they gave all workers a flat increase in pay of 14/- a week, which amounted to an increase of $3\frac{1}{2}$ per cent (but would be $7\frac{1}{2}$ per cent for the lowest paid workers) with a likely extra $1\frac{1}{2}$ per cent wage drift from local bargaining, making 5 per cent in all, this promised little curb on the expected inflationary rise of pay. Whitehall opinion was reported as extremely sceptical as to the possibility of the T.U.C. carrying out an effective voluntary policy on this basis, and it was unclear from statements made by the Prime Minister and the Secretary for Economic Affairs whether the $3\frac{1}{2}$ per cent norm suggested by the T.U.C. was accepted as a realistic figure. Rumour began to build up that the Government would have to take drastic measures to succeed in holding pay and prices down. In the event, the representatives of the trade-union executives by giving the report a majority of only 536,000 out of 9,240,000, demonstrated their reluctance to accept the limitations of even the moderate degree of restraint proposed by the General Council, thus leaving the Government with a clear responsibility to act. It was precisely this situation that George Woodcock had sought to persuade the union executives to avoid bringing about. He argued, 'It was better for trade unionists to be dealing with trade-union problems than to allow some outsider to do it.'

The failure of the T.U.C. to secure the support of its affiliated unions so as to enable the General Council to administer a voluntary incomes policy effectively, is a reflection of the fundamental problem that has remained unresolved during the whole period of its existence. In 1874 a resolution proposing that the Parliamentary Committee should be given federal powers was discussed, but nothing came of this proposal, nor of others like it, until the General Federation of Trade Unions was established in 1899. This organisation failed to realise the hopes of its sponsors and accomplished relatively little. An attempt was made after the reorganisation in 1921 to give the General Council greater power and authority, but this foundered on the General Strike. Since the Second World War the unions have been prepared to give the General Council a greater measure of authority in certain limited respects, for example, to intervene when inter-union disputes or the activities of a single union threaten to have adverse repercussions on the trade-union movement as a whole.

The General Council has in practice been extremely reluctant to seek the extension of its own authority and it has been most cautious in exercising the powers that it constitutionally enjoys. Behind the reluctance of the General Council to give a more positive lead lies a number of deeper conflicts that perpetually hobble the trade unions. Perhaps the most important of these factors are the divisions of interest that cut deeply across the structure of the trade-union movement. There is a common tendency to see the trade unions as homogeneous bodies protecting the common interest of the worker against that of the employer. This concept of the trade unions has much truth in it, but it is also false in important respects.

On issues of economic, social and political interest, the trade unions and their members are sharply divided. The unions of white-collar workers, and those composed mainly of highly skilled workers, have different interests from those which organise mostly unskilled workers. The conflict comes out extremely clearly in wage claims. Highly skilled, and administrative and technician grades desire to widen their differentials and they are not prepared to accept wage-restraint policies which might jeopardise the pay differentials to which they believe strongly they are morally entitled. Low-paid workers believe equally strongly they are justified in improving their relative pay. In this situation there is little chance of voluntarily maintaining a stable situation.

3. THE PROBLEM OF TRADE UNION STRUCTURE

The untidy structure pattern of the trade unions in Britain has long been recognised as a major handicap to the development and and the carrying out of an effective central policy. In 1962 the Trades Union Congress passed a resolution stating that 'It is time the British Trade Union movement adapted its structure to modern conditions.' Mr. George Woodcock, who welcomed this decision as 'the beginning of a tremendous undertaking', had made up his mind after a visit to Sweden, to try to achieve what two previous attempts to reform trade union structure had failed to achieve.

The objective of the General Secretary of the T.U.C. was to bring about the gradual reorganisation of the trade unions on broad industrial lines as accomplished in Sweden. It had taken the Swedes thirty years to achieve this result, and Woodcock was under no illusion that it would be brought about in a short time in Britain. He did believe, however, that it might be possible to persuade the unions to accept the need to achieve a more rational union structure as a long run aim. The optimism of the General Secretary was soon found to rest on nothing more substantial than a hope that the unions would be willing to move gradually towards a new pattern of trade unionism. When it came to the vote, the General Council left its General Secretary as the lone supporter of the idea of adopting industrial unionism as the specific objective of T.U.C. policy. The report of General Council on its enquiry into the structure of the unions stated categorically, for the third time since 1921, that 'Basic alteration in union structure is impracticable' and 'no comprehensive scheme of widespread structural reform' possible.

The General Secretary made the best of the situation, informing Congress that the General Council would take an active role in seeking to bring about amalgamation between unions with similar trade interests, and failing that the extension of federations of unions. During the next few years there were to be a substantial number of amalgamations, including those of the Foundry Workers with the A.E.U., the A.S.S.E.T. and the Scientific Workers, the London Society of Compositors and the Typographical Association.

The Amalgamations brought about and encouraged by T.U.C. support have undoubtedly been to some advantage, but the fundamental problems remain. Over two thirds of the affiliated trade union membership is now concentrated in eighteen unions, each with a membership of over 100,000. Six unions have over one half of the membership, and three unions are in the super size class with memberships of eight hundred thousand, one million and one million and a half. At the other end of the scale, there are some eighty small organisations each with fewer than 5000 members; outside of the T.U.C. there is a much larger number of small unions.

Unfortunately, the natural growth of trade unions by recruitment of new members and by amalgamation is not producing a more rational structure, as the Congress tacitly recognised when it authorised the Council to conduct the enquiry in 1962.

The impossibility of making progress in the direction of industrial unionism has led Professor Turner to propose the amalgamation of the big three as an alternative way of going forward. Since it is the existence of the big, multi-occupation, multi-industry unions that constitute the pivotal obstacle to union structural reform, the amalgamation of the A.E.U., N.U.G.M.W., and T.G.W.U. would remove this difficulty at one stroke.

Such an amalgamation would transform the T.U.C.: with three-eighths of the latter's total affiliation it would almost certainly dominate Congress itself, and even with the T.U.C. General Council's present composition, would command a single block of one quarter of that august body's members; though it might also give the General Council and its staff a new standing as the protectors of small union interests – and by comparison all other British unions would certainly be small. Most important, it would enormously reinforce the T.U.C.'s effective authority without raising the awkward question of the latter's formal powers, since the merger's massive presence in nearly every major sector of employment would ensure that the T.U.C. decision to which it subscribed (and one cannot imagine that the T.U.C. would make many decisions to which it did not) was, if not automatically implemented, at least formidably supported at the industrial level.[1]

If Professor Turner's proposal were to be implemented, and discussions between the' big three' suggest that the idea is not as fanciful as at first sight it might seem, it would have major repercussions. It would certainly do much to overcome the problem of multi-union representation in manufacturing industry and it would be an important contribution towards a solution of the problem that now exists in the reconciling of workshop bargaining with the requirements of a national incomes policy.

The growth of workshop bargaining has exposed the weakness of the T.U.C.'s policy of encouraging the development of federations of trade unions as a solution to the problem of overlapping unions. The creation of trade-union federations made it possible for unions to negotiate industry-wide national agreements with employers' associations, but the limitation of the organisation of the federations to the carrying out of this function has contributed to the divorce of workplace bargaining from the national negotiating machinery.

An extension of the authority and organisational arrangements of the present federations would in effect be to achieve industrial unionism. It was precisely this development that led the authors of an earlier report on trade-union structure to see federations as a half-way house to industrial organisation. The failure of the federations to extend beyond the half-way-house stage indicates that the big general unions are not prepared to accept the logic of this development since it implies their disintegration.

The only practicable alternative to the amalgamation proposal made by Professor Turner, which would provide a solution to the multi-union representation and hence independent joint shop steward organisation at the place of work, would be for the major unions to agree to adopt the American principle of exclusive plant representation. This would involve the major unions agreeing to accept sole responsibility for organising and servicing members at

[1] H. A. Turner, 'British Trade Union Structure: A New Approach', *British Journal of Industrial Relations*, vol. ii, no. 2 (Jul 1964).

particular plants or enterprises. For example, it might be agreed that the T.G.W.U. was entirely responsible for negotiations at plant A and that the other unions would cease to recruit there. At Plant B the N.U.G.M.W. would have the responsibility and at plant C the A.E.U. All new employees who had not been in a union would join the union with the bargaining responsibility. The other unions would pay to the union with bargaining responsibility an agreed proportion of the contributions of their members as a service fee. In this way it would be possible to link workplace bargaining much more closely to national bargaining and to the obligations entered into by the unions at national level. It would not be easy to agree on a distribution of bargaining jurisdictions, but it could be done by the unions – if they would agree – with the help of the T.U.C.

4. THE GROWTH OF WHITE COLLAR WORKERS

By 1980 there will be substantially more people employed in clerical, technical, administrative jobs and in service and professional employment, than in the traditional types of manual employment. This change in the occupational pattern of the labour force carries with it considerable implications for the trade unions in the future. During the past century, the trade-union movement has been dominated by unions in coal, textiles, railways and ship-building and engineering. With the exception of the engineering, which has diversified into a myriad of new industries, all of the traditionally highly unionised industries have declined tremendously as employers of labour. If, therefore, the unions are to maintain their numerical strength they must replace the members they are losing in the traditional sectors with recruits from the rapidly expanding areas of employment.

In the past twenty years, there have been spectacular developments in some areas of 'white-collar' employment, in other areas they have been much less successful. Overall during this time, the unions have greatly increased their membership among white collar workers, but they have done no more in proportionate terms than keep pace with the rise in the total numbers. The most highly organised sector is public employment, namely, national and local government, nationalised industries, the health service and education. Considerable success has also been achieved in the organisation of technicians, bank clerks and employees in films, broadcasting and television.

The growth of unions organising in these rapidly expanding 'white-collar' occupations has been viewed with suspicion and trepidation by many of the trade unionists from the traditional fields of union organisation. At the T.U.C. there has been great reluctance to adjust the membership of the General Council so that it fully reflects the changing membership pattern of the unions.

At the time of the pay pause, there appeared to be some possibility that the large 'white-collar' unions not affiliated to the T.U.C., namely National and Local Government Officers' Association, the National Union of Teachers and others would form a separate 'white-collar union' centre as exists in the Scandinavian countries. Any possibility of this happening was eliminated when the membership of NALGO decided to affiliate to the T.U.C. It is generally believed that sooner or later the N.U.T. will also join the T.U.C.

The 'white-collar' unions are now exercising a growing influence in the T.U.C. Twenty years ago they made little impact on the Congress or the General Council. Today, their influence at Congress is considerable. They are now responsible for a large number of the most important motions and their representatives have become a powerful, if not yet dominant, voice in Congress debates. On the General Council, the weight of tradition and organisational inertia restricts their influence, but it would seem to be only a matter of time before they become a powerful element in that body.

5. THE T.U.C. AND UNION DEMOCRACY

In the duties of the General Council laid down in the constitution of the T.U.C. there is no reference to any responsibility for intervening in any conflict of interest between a member or group of members and the union to which they belong. Under the 'Bridlington Rules' the right of a member to transfer from one organisation to another is regulated in the interest of orderly trade-union recruitment and good inter-union relations. But under these rules an individual may suffer if he is expelled against his wishes, or is refused entry to a union under arrangements made to prevent inter-union competition.[1]

[1] See S. W. Lerner, *Breakaway Unions and the Small Trade Union* (1961).

The T.U.C. is empowered to intervene in the affairs of an affiliated union 'if at any time there appears to the General Council to be justification for an investigation into the conduct of any affiliated organisation on the ground that the activities of such organisation are detrimental to the interests of the Trade Union Movement or contrary to the declared interests of the Congress . . .'.

Under this rule the General Council has a wide latitude, but it has exercised its discretion in an ultra-cautious fashion. In the E.T.U. case it was most reluctant to intervene, even though the situation had become a matter of public scandal. In its evidence to the Royal Commission the General Council admit to there 'being prima facie evidence' that the E.T.U. had a case to answer, but justify its failure to act on the grounds that 'when an individual member of a union, or a newspaper, makes allegations against an affiliated union which that union rejects as untrue, the General Council cannot assume that more credence should be given to the charge than to its rejection by the union.'

The problem of protecting union members when officers on committees of the union deprive them of their rights is one that has given considerable concern as the result of a number of cases that have come before the Courts in the past twenty years. The Courts have shown that they are ready to intervene to protect the individual in cases of wrongful expulsion, electoral malpractice or other irregularity in the conduct of a union's affairs. However, as the Ministry of Labour noted in its evidence to the Royal Commission, 'The law does not . . . protect the union member completely from suffering injustice at the hands of the union and, when it does, the process may be long and expensive.'

This relative lack of legal protection, as the Ministry observe, 'Derives largely from the fact that unions have been viewed as voluntary associations in whose internal affairs the courts should not normally interfere.' The T.U.C. believes that there should be no change in this situation. In its evidence to the Royal Commission it opposed suggestions that the Registrar should be given powers to insist that the rules of the union should conform to approved standards, or that he or an outside body should be empowered to intervene in cases of complaint that the rules had been broken or misapplied.

The General Council was prepared, albeit tentatively, to consider performing an appeals function, if this was desired by member unions, though it did not put this forward as a positive proposal. In this respect it is of interest that the Irish Congress of Trade Unions established an Appeals Board in 1963. Members of all unions affiliated to the Congress are entitled to use this machinery either as individuals or as groups. However, individuals may only bring complaints about wrongful expulsion, but a group of members are allowed to bring complaints against their union on a wider range of issues. In the first five years of its existence the Board dealt with some thirty-eight cases. According to one observer, 'the results have not been spectacular' but the Board does appear to have served a useful if limited purpose.[1]

It is no doubt the case that in general trade unions are very careful to observe their rules, but it is inevitable that cases will arise when rules are wilfully broken, or perhaps more frequently, simply misunderstood or misapplied. It would, therefore, add to public confidence in the unions if they were to make provision for the T.U.C. to set up an impartial appeals board. It may well be, however, that the Royal Commission will conclude that the T.U.C. has had ample time to establish an appeals procedure, and decide to recommend that the Government should take the steps necessary to give union members this type of protection.

6. THE FUTURE PATTERN OF INDUSTRIAL RELATIONS

The problem of most important contemporary significance is undoubtedly the growth of local bargaining and with it the emergence of the unofficial strike as a feature of the industrial relations system.

One of the suggestions before the Royal Commission is that collective agreements should be made into collective contracts which would be legally binding upon the parties. Such a step would then make unions and employers liable to pay damages if they were responsible for going on strike in breach of the agreement. Thus the unions would have to take steps to ensure that their agents observed the agreement. Whether a step of this kind would entirely prevent unofficial strikes is open to doubt, but it would certainly have an important effect on collective bargaining. It would almost certainly lead to a distinction being made between

[1] K. I. Sams, 'The Appeals Board of the Irish Congress of Trade Unions', *British Journal of Industrial Relations* (Jul 1968).

disputes of interests – concerning the making of the contract – and disputes of rights arising out of the contract. It would also lead to agreements being made for a particular time period; to the details being fully spelled out; and to the development of a grievance arbitration system.

Proposals for a change in the law are anathema to the T.U.C. which is absolutely against any suggestion that the law relating to collective bargaining should be altered. In its evidence to the Royal Commission the T.U.C. rejected completely the notion that strikes could be prevented by any legal device such as a compulsory strike ballot or cooling-off period. The traditional industrial relations system based upon the concept that trade unions and employers should be free to settle their own affairs with the minimum of legal intervention was defended vigorously.

Some unions have argued that the law should be changed so as to give positive support to organisations that are refused recognition by an employer, although they have recruited a substantial number of his employees. The T.U.C., consistent with its view that the law should be kept out of industrial relations, saw a danger in this idea and argued that the absence of any assistance from the law had been of great benefit to the unions.

The fact that trade unions in Britain have succeeded through their own efforts in strengthening their organisation and in obtaining recognition, not relying on the assistance of Government through legislation, is one of the most important factors sustaining their strength and independence. Trade Unions have not been given privileges; they have fought for what they have achieved. If they had been granted privileges, if their organisation had been sustained and strengthened by Government action, it might well be logical to argue today that trade union function would also be the responsibility of Government; the right to bargain had been granted by Government and Government could take it away. Trade union strength has been developed without the help of any exernal agency.[1]

The basic concept of the system of industrial relations defended by the T.U.C. is that the state should hold the ring while the two sides of industry fight each other until they reach an accommodation. Where it is necessary for the state to intervene, as it might

[1] T.U.C. Evidence to the Royal Commission on Trade Unions and Employers' Associations.

be necessary when the balance of power suffers from a permanent disequilibrium owing to a major weakness of one of the parties, the role of the state should be to act as crutch, to support and assist, not to supersede.

The difficulty with the power-bargaining concept of industrial relations is that it requires a fine balance otherwise it works too strongly in favour of one side or the other. It also presupposes a relatively static situation in which the issues that are in dispute remain relatively simple and are well understood by both sides. In rapidly changing situations and under modern technological, economic and social conditions, the costs of adjustment implicit in power bargaining may be greater than a society is prepared to tolerate.

Since this concept of industrial relations which is held by the T.U.C. and by a substantial proportion of the trade unions and employers has proved to be no longer compatible with the maintenance of full employment, high rates of economic growth and a stable balance of payments, it will inevitably have to be modified. Although totalitarian forms of socialism are not acceptable in Britain, the Government is playing a much larger role than in the past, and it is unlikely that this will diminish. This means that it will not be able to leave unions and employers free to settle their affairs without regard for the way in which they influence and determine the goals set by the Government and approved by the community in general.

The problem is to work out a new balance in the tripartite relation between Government, employers and unions. The refusal of the unions to give the T.U.C. greater authority will inevitably have the effect of diminishing their sphere of freedom, since in the last resort the Government will have to take the steps necessary to protect the interests of the community where it is clear that the behaviour of unions and employers is jeopardising those interests.

7. RELATIONS WITH THE LABOUR PARTY

In developing its future role in relation to Government and to its constituent unions, the T.U.C. may have to face the fact that the links between the trade unions and the Labour Party may be different in the future from what they have been for the past sixty-odd years. All the signs point to a weakening of the Labour alliance and a gradual shift towards a position of neutrality in the future.

This major change in the structure of British politics is being brought about by a number of factors. Economic prosperity and rising standards of living are tending to blur the difference between the parties in terms of social class. As the pattern of party support changes so too does the pattern of trade union membership. As the number of 'white collar' trade unionists increase the already substantial support for the Conservative Party among trade unionists is likely to grow larger.

What is also of considerable importance is the gradual realisation, especially among younger trade unionists, that in most respects it really makes little difference whether the Labour Party or the Conservative Party is in power. The present General Secretary and his two predecessors have all stated that the role of the T.U.C is the same whichever party is in power. The T.U.C. expects to enjoy a closer and more co-operative relationship with a Labour Government than with a Conservative one, and to some extent this has been borne out, but in most respects the T.U.C. has enjoyed no special advantage.

The difficulties which have arisen in connection with the administration of a national incomes policy have certainly been no easier since 1964, than before the Labour Party was returned to office. It is, in fact, likely that a Conservative Party with its greater support for a market economy may have less conflict with the unions in the future than the Labour Party. There is a fundamental incompatibility between the T.U.C. with its strong attachment to union autonomy and the type of planned socialism which is the ultimate ideal of many members of the Labour Party. This conflict lies dormant when the Labour Party is out of office, but when it is in power and seeks to achieve its goals, it is inevitably in conflict with the unions.

Even if a Labour Government advances no closer to socialism than a Conservative Government, it is bound to run into problems with the trade unions, simply because it must govern in the interests of the whole community and not just to suit the unions. Since, however, the unions have a greater expectation from a Labour Government than from a Conservative one, their sense of disappointment and dissatisfaction is the greater.

If the unions were to occupy a more neutral and central position, and if at the same time the trade-union movement covered a much broader section of the employed labour force than the 43 per cent in trade unions today, they might well be more influential in the future than they have been in the past. If they could achieve the status and carry out the functions in the British economy envisaged by Mr. George Woodcock, their role would grow. If on the other hand they fail to seize the opportunity and shrink from giving the T.U.C. the power it needs, the role of the Government will become much more dominant and that of the unions will diminish.

8. DEVELOPMENTS IN THE WORK OF THE T.U.C.

Whatever happens in the immediate future to its relationship to the Labour Party, the function of the T.U.C. will continue to be to act as a union of the unions, to promote their interests as effectively as possible. The success of the T.U.C. will depend to no small extent on its leadership and on its organisational structure. It is generally agreed that the T.U.C. is an efficient, well run organisation, but the extension of its work in connection with the vetting of wage claims has clearly taxed its capacity to the limit. The plain fact of the matter is that it operates on too small a budget and provides too limited services to make the decisive impact on trade union affairs that is now required.

If the T.U.C. is really to make a complete success of its wages policy, it will need to employ a much larger staff on this aspect of the work. The problem of investigation and administration will grow considerably as productivity bargaining expands. The T.U.C. will not know what is taking place unless it is able to obtain information direct from the union officers at the enterprise.

More than twenty-five years ago, it was suggested that the T.U.C. should open Regional Offices. In the carrying out of its functions today, Regional Offices are essential. They would, of course, be expensive to run, and the necessary finance would have to be raised from higher affiliation fees. Though the unions paying these fees might not agree, the annual fee of 1s. 6d. per member is ludicrously small. It brings in some £500,000, of which £160,000 is remitted to the I.C.F.T.U. and other bodies. Most of the trade-union centres in comparable countries such as Sweden, Germany and the U.S.A. enjoy a much larger income.

The T.U.C. is spending more money on education than ever before, but the amount that needs to be spent is far greater. It has become vitally important that the T.U.C. explains its policy directly to union members. One of the main reasons why the Swedish trade-union centre secures the support of its affiliated membership is because of the tremendous efforts made to ensure that active trade unionists understand the policy of the central body.

The only major, and perhaps the most important development made by the T.U.C. in its service function in the post-war period, has been the establishment of a Production Department. This department has done a great deal to make trade-union officials and shop stewards aware of the opportunities that lie in increasing productivity. In its evidence to the Royal Commission, the T.U.C. stated: 'The Production Department endeavours to bring about new attitudes by relating workers' interests to particular techniques in order to show how disadvantages can be avoided or mitigated, while benefits can be secured for workers.' Productivity bargaining has greatly increased the need for this type of service.

Since the T.U.C. started its wage-vetting activity, it has considerably expanded its Economic Department. The Department's main responsibility is to service the Economic Committee, the Nationalised Industries Committee and the Wages Policy Committee of the General Council. It is also responsible for servicing the representatives of the T.U.C. on the National Economic Development Council. The work of this Department has grown considerably and the staff has expanded to almost a dozen, all of whom are graduates in economics or an allied subject and most of whom have had some experience in industry. The staff of the Department will certainly have to be expanded further if the T.U.C. becomes further involved in the administration of an incomes policy – especially if this requires investigation and analysis of productivity bargaining.

The other departments of the T.U.C., namely, International, Organisation and Social Insurance are all run on a tight budget which severely limits their activity. There can be no doubt that affiliated unions obtain an excellent service from the Departments of the T.U.C., but if the T.U.C. is to measure up to the opportunities that lie before it there will have to be a considerable expansion of its activities and its organisation.

Mr. George Woodcock said, when commending the decision of the Congress in 1962 to embark on the study of trade-union organisation, that 'structure was a function of purpose'. The purpose of trade unions had to be examined afresh in the context of a modern society and their structure had to be adapted to enable them to achieve that purpose. In the light of the extremely modest developments in the organisation of the T.U.C. itself, it would seem that Mr. Woodcock has been unable to apply his own doctrine.

Here lies the challenge of the future. Can the T.U.C. develop its authority and its organisation so as to exercise the dominating role that it must play if it is to carry out the kind of purpose envisaged for it by its General Secretary? If it is to be a genuine estate of the realm, exercising responsibility for a vital part of our economic activity, then it must make the adaptations that are necessary to meet the challenge of the next 100 years. It remains to be seen whether the unions will find the vitality, the wisdom and the determination to achieve the changes that will be required.

Index